THE COMMUNICATING MANAGER

Mike Dutfield has been in management training for 24 years, and has worked for many of the major multinationals (including Philips, Lyons Tetley and Honeywell) as well as in the public sector as a Lecturer in Organisational Development at Birmingham Polytechnic.

Chris Eling is a social scientist and engineer with many years experience in management training. For the past five years, Chris and Mike have been partners in their own organisation consultancy, running a range of courses on interviewing and counselling skills.

THE COMMUNICATING MANAGER

A GUIDE TO

WORKING EFFECTIVELY

WITH PEOPLE

Mike Dutfield
Chris Eling

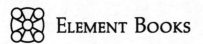 ELEMENT BOOKS

First published in Great Britain in 1990 by
Element Books Limited
Longmead, Shaftesbury, Dorset

Designed by Jenny Liddle
Cover design by Max Fairbrother
Cover illustration by David Sim
Typeset by Poole Typesetting (Wessex) Ltd., Bournemouth
Printed and bound in Great Britain by
Billings, Hylton Road, Worcester

British Library Cataloguing in Publication Data
Dutfield, Mike
The communicating manager: a guide to working effectively with people
1. Personnel management. Counselling. Interviewing
I. Title II. Eling, Chris
658.385

ISBN 1-85230-080-9

To Becca, Chloe, Fred and Sam
in the hope that they enjoy
learning as much as we do

CONTENTS

Acknowledgements   viii
Introduction   1

Part 1: A Model for Successful
Interpersonal Management

1 A Practical Model for Effective Communication   7
2 Purposeful Communication   19
3 Planning Communication   29
4 The Right Role for the Job   34
5 Values, Attitudes, Needs and Expectations   43
6 Pressures and Influences in Communication   50
7 Communication Skills   64
Summary of the Interviewing Model   79

Part 2: Bringing about Change
through Other People

8 Managing Change   83
9 Handling Redundancy   99
10 Effective Appraisals   122
11 The Counselling Manager   149
12 Reviewing Work   174
Manager's Preparation Document   221

Bibliography   223
Contact Address   224

Acknowledgements

We would like to thank Judy Stewart, for without her help and support our long-held wish to write a book would not have been translated into action and finally into a finished product. She, along with John Watts, also read our first draft, and their comments, both on the writing and the content were most valuable. Trevor Dixon's contribution to some of the case material was also very helpful.

It now seems a long while ago that we met Sheila Forbes, now of Storehouse, Frank Hayter, of Philips Electronics and Charles Napier, now of Lyons Tetley, to design a course on managerial interviewing. Without them, the subsequent courses and this book would not have been possible. We would also thank all our past and present colleagues who have worked with us on interviewing skills courses, particularly Bob Havard and Judy Stewart, for the contributions they have made to developing our ideas.

Most of all we would thank our numerous course participants, who have ensured our thoughts have continued to be practical and relevant to current managerial situations. They are also the source of the majority of the case material in the book.

Finally we would like to thank Gill and Jackie for the various forms of help they have provided, while we struggled to put pen to paper.

M.D. *and* C.E.

Introduction

Why should busy managers read this book?

We know that many people are initially employed to 'do' a particular job; they are employed for their specialist knowledge or skill, and as they become more senior in the organisation they spend less and less time 'doing', and more time talking to people in order to do their job. Of course there are jobs in which talking to others is the core skill right from the start. Typically salesmen and personnel people spend a high percentage of their time talking to people, but many specialists – engineers, scientists, computer experts, planners – may spend much more of their time 'doing' the job they are employed to do, and often regard anyone coming to talk to them as an interruption of their real work.

Certainly promotion to a supervision or management job almost certainly means that a higher percentage of time is spent talking to people. It means that work has to be allocated, checked and improved, and that all those difficult problems that people bring with them – like absenteeism, lateness, personal difficulties and career aspirations – have to be dealt with. In many cases promotion, whilst it does not mean managing staff, will mean increased responsibility and having to deal with more senior staff within the organisation, or people outside of the organisation who are important to its success. This is not a new insight. Indeed Rosemary Stewart looked at the contact patterns of British managers back in 1967. Her studies identified that for many managers the majority of their working time was spent in what they saw as meetings. They were generally communicating with a member of staff in such activities as checking that work was up to standard, monitoring work to ensure that it would be on time, or negotiating for resources. We see no evidence to suggest that this has changed since Stewart did her original work. In the introduction to the second edition, published in 1988, she claims her findings are still relevant to understanding what managers do. Indeed from our consultancy and training work it is evident that with the reduction in overheads and increased competition, the ability to manage these interactions probably has greater importance in terms of business effectiveness.

We have found from a survey undertaken with one of our client companies that managers spend between 30 and 95 per cent of their time 'interviewing', as we have called all one-to-one communications in work. It is not surprising that they want to improve the effectiveness of that time.

Typically the interviews with which they want help are:

- How to let my staff know what they are good at and what they are not so good at.
- Motivating my staff to work harder.
- Helping my specialists realise what effect their work is having on other people.
- Persuading service departments to do work for me when they still have work to do for someone else.
- Handling conflicts when customers have different priorities.
- How to get my staff to improve their performance without resorting to the disciplinary procedure.
- How to get other people to recognise that they need to change.
- How to get clients and customers to recognise what I, as a specialist, have to offer.
- The tough interviews – discipline, termination, and redundancy.
- Managing career aspirations.
- Helping people at work deal with personal problems.
- Handling complaints.
- Ensuring standards are met when I do not have direct control, and indeed may have to tackle someone more senior than me.

We will not deal with all these situations in the book, but we think that you will see that the ideas which we put forward will help with these and many other interviews.

Of course these are very different situations, and we recognise that the way they are dealt with in different organisations will vary, but we have found that our approach has worked with people from very different backgrounds, in very different jobs. It is a practical approach which will provide you with a means of analysing the requirements of any interview and devising an appropriate plan of action. It will also provide you with a means of reviewing your interviews so that you can continue to monitor and improve your effectiveness. It will provide you with practical ways of getting more out of the time you spend in interviews, and will, through the

A PROFILE OF YOUR INTERVIEWS – WHY DO YOU
TALK TO OTHERS IN YOUR JOB?

Here is a list of reasons for holding interviews. It is not an
exhaustive list, so add to it if you feel that your own reasons
are not covered. What percentage of your interviewing time
do you spend on each of these? Try to think of an example in
the categories which are relevant to your job:

1. Managing staff...%

2. Problem-solving...%

3. Giving information and advice....................................%

4. Obtaining information...%

5. Reaching agreements..%

6. Maintaining relationships...%

7. ....%

use of transcripts of real interviews, enable you to benefit from
other people's methods. Our central theme throughout the book
will be to invite you to consider how you can use your skills most
effectively. This book will not set out to tell you the one best way
to conduct a particular interview but to invite you to use the tools
we provide so that you can improve the use of your skills.

How to use the book

We have already said that our approach to interviewing is practical;
it is therefore important that this book is practical for its intended
readers. We are aware as professional trainers that not all participants enter a training course with exactly the same need or levels of
knowledge. Readers of management books are no different and it
may not be appropriate for all to read the book from beginning to
end, in the sequence in which it is written.

To deal with this problem we have written the book in two parts.
Part 1 builds up the model which managers have found so helpful
for managing successful interpersonal situations. Once you are
familiar with it, the model will help you decide what needs to be

done, and will provide you with a simple and quick planning
method which is applicable to all interviews.

Part 2 focuses on the central issue of bringing about change
through other people, and looks particularly at:

- Introducing change.
- Regular review of work, and setting standards.
- The formal appraisal or performance review.
- Handling redundancy – announcing the fact, and counsell-
  ing and supporting the employee.

In these chapters you will find transcripts of interviews which have
been successful, and some where the interviewer has got into some
of the typical difficulties. Alongside each of these transcripts you
will find our comments analysing the interviews, with our suggestions for improvement. There are also outlines for a number of
approaches, so that you can choose one which suits your style and
skills, and which is appropriate for your particular circumstances.
Each section will also provide you with practical exercises to help
you relate the ideas to your work.

It is our suggestion that if your interest is in interviewing generally you should initially concentrate on Part 1. This may be the best
place to start for the younger or less experienced manager. On the
other hand the experienced manager may prefer to start with Part 2,
referring back to Part 1 for extra clarification or detail about the
ideas. Of course these are only suggestions; if you bought the book
because you have your first appraisal interview next week, the
chapter on appraisal interviewing would be a good place to start.

Most of the managers we have on our courses are men, and we
do tend to write our case studies as if both people are men. We have
used 'he' and 'she' and 'they' meaning both men and women.

Part One

A Model for Successful Interpersonal Management

————————————————————▶

A Practical Model
for Effective Communication

Over ten years ago we were working in the field of Management Development and Training in a multinational electronics company. It was a company that was rightly proud of the quality of its management training and saw itself as one of the leading companies in this country in terms of the way it treated its staff and managers. The management was involved in trying to participate with its workforce and there were a number of job-enrichment and work-structuring projects. The company was investing heavily in management and supervisory training. The vast majority of their establishments would have had their own lower management and supervisory training courses, and these were supported centrally by a whole series of other programmes. While a number of these courses concentrated on the knowledge or techniques of management, such as budgeting and financial controls, there was emphasis on 'people management', mainly through general management courses, with a particular interest in the understanding and management of groups. Despite all this effort, or perhaps because of the increased knowledge and awareness of the managers, a further need was perceived.

In the main, managers were appreciative of what they had received and had been able to use much of it in their jobs, but they started to recognise there was a whole range of work situations that had been ignored. For example, whilst knowing the theories of motivation, they were still unsure how to actually get staff to work harder. Sometimes they had been able to apply the ideas with one member of staff but not with another. Others wanted to know how to get their specialists to see the effect they were having on other people. Sometimes the need was solving problems with other departmental managers.

Gradually some common threads started to emerge and the need was identified as 'how to manage events or interviews with another person (for example, boss, subordinate, colleague, supplier, etc.) with whom I already have a working relationship, to achieve some work purpose more effectively'. What managers wanted to achieve varied enormously. In relation to their subordinates it included, on the one hand, such things as making people redundant, or disciplining them, and, on the other hand, issues like helping people to solve personal problems or supporting them through career changes. The key question was 'How should I do it?' In other words they wanted practical help, not theory. In addition the 'how' had to be achievable in a way that recognised that there was a working relationship between the people and that, in most cases, they would have to go on working together.

When we started researching this area we found that we were not dealing with a unique situation. Rosemary Stewart had identified contact patterns of managers, and our findings did not significantly differ from hers. Her studies identified that most managerial working time was spent in these, largely one-to-one, situations dealing with similar issues. We see no evidence in organisations today to suggest that these findings have significantly changed.

Over the years we have been involved in training managers, in a wide range of industrial and commercial companies, and also in public sector organisations, we have reached a number of general conclusions.

Most managers are good at handling some situations, but they are likely to be weaker at handling others. In other words we are not talking about good and bad managers, but rather the ability to handle a wide variety of situations. Certainly the successful manager's range may be greater than the less successful manager's. In fact he may be better in all situations, but that is not the point. What we have found is that even a successful or competent manager will be less effective at dealing with certain issues than others. On the other hand, a rewarding experience for us as trainers is to work with a manager who struggles with many interpersonal situations, and find that he is outstandingly good at one or two. The fact that even competent managers are less effective at some situations than others is clearly a statement of the obvious, but it is surprising how often the judgements made of people end up being so generalised that they are seen as good or bad at everything.

Despite the time managers spend on one-to-one communications, the time is not necessarily usefully spent. We are not saying that there is a direct correlation between time and effectiveness, but frequently with clarity of purpose, and good use of skill, time can be saved without losing effectiveness.

In recent years we have been struck by the increasing interest in Total Quality Control in British industry. Certainly as a consumer the notion of zero defects is attractive. Who wants to buy a television only to find that it does not work? If one does have that misfortune, not only do one's feelings about the product and its maker change, but one also understands the importance of the Company Wide Quality concept of 'getting it right first time' as one experiences the inconvenience and cost of remedying faults.

What strikes us particularly is that as consumers we are not prepared to accept this inconvenience as reasonable, or normal, and would subscribe to the quality improvement concepts. Indeed in increasing numbers, we are introducing them into organisations to improve the quality of products, and services. But what about ourselves and the way we work? How many of us regularly sit through meetings where the same things are discussed every week, without reaching a decision? Or spend two hours in a meeting when we know the business could be completed in half an hour? Certainly in a lot of interviews, getting it right first time is critical. This is particularly true in selection interviews where you can miss a suitable candidate, or put a candidate off working for you, or alternatively not get the job. However it also applies in a whole range of other interviews. Take as an example an appraisal interview; you have a subordinate who is basically sound, he almost certainly could do a bigger job, as long as he improves in a particular area of work. If your subordinate leaves the interview without a balanced view of his performance, including his strengths and areas for improvement and how he should work on those in the future, you will have a problem. If he leaves having only heard about his abilities to do a bigger job, his unreal expectations of the future will make it more difficult for him, in the future, to receive the feed-back about necessary improvements. Conversely if your subordinate leaves with the impression that his performance is inadequate, having only heard the criticism, you will probably have a demotivated member of staff to manage, who also does not think much of appraisal schemes! This is nearly as bad as the colleague of ours who said to us recently, 'I think I had my appraisal last week'! Obviously we have oversimplified the example, but it is true that in many human interactions the cost of not getting it right first time is not just that there is no positive benefit, but a negative response is created. You are frequently in a worse position than when you started.

The approach that we have developed over more than ten years has given managers the opportunity to "get it right". But if it is self-evident that managers should be clear what they are doing and be better prepared, what is it that stops them being as effective as they might be? **What stops you being as effective as you might be?**

Why things go wrong

Do you sometimes go to a meeting with someone, spend an hour with them, and then, only as you are walking down the corridor afterwards, remember what you went to see them about? Do you have a meeting with a senior colleague, and afterwards say to yourself, 'Well it's so obvious I cannot understand why he can't see it.' Do you hear people say, 'Well it's not my job to tell him!'? As the boss, do you sometimes catch yourself saying, in effect, to a questioning subordinate, 'Because *I'm the Boss*'. Or do you sometimes find that even though you've explained things perfectly well, they've done exactly the opposite? These, and many other frustrating experiences, are not unusual, and we have noticed that there are usually good reasons for them which can be managed.

RELYING ON RATIONALITY

It may be our particular experience, because we have worked with a large number of science- or engineering-based companies, but one of the problems is the reliance people put on the 'rational'. Managers know that people do not always behave in logical ways, but it does not stop them explaining things by 'presenting the facts' and expecting that to be good enough. The assumption seems to be that if you tell someone the facts, they will automatically come to the same conclusion as you. We even found this when we were teaching management to some social workers, who were well used to dealing with people, and indeed very skilled in their social worker role. When promoted, they seemed to assume that management meant hard-headed rationality. It was as if all the messy human stuff, like not being interested, being preoccupied with something else, or simply being inconsistent, was no longer relevant.

There have been many influences that have led managers to think that there should be some way of quantifying and measuring everything, and that this measurement and analysis will provide the answers. We are not against measurement and analysis, but often when we are dealing with human beings, face to face, the analysis becomes so complex that it is not useful in practice. At the same time, because managers know that dealing with people can be difficult and complex, they often fall back on the ideas of rationality with which they are familiar and more comfortable.

On our training courses we often provide managers with the tools to analyse a wide range of personal characteristics for a selection interview, or they are asked to assess a range of characteristics to award a salary increase based on performance. It is not unusual to see managers massaging the 'rational' data to confirm what they first thought, or blaming the tool when it does not confirm what they know, but being convinced that they are being quite rational. In one company we developed an appraisal system which did not have the apparently analytical process of ticking boxes and totalling scores, but required managers to make an overall judgement based on a lengthy discussion with the subordinate. What we found was that a considerable number of managers needed the comfort of the 'rational' method, and developed their own box-ticking method to support the judgements.

Peters and Waterman in their book *In Search of Excellence* blame much of this emphasis on the rational on the education provided by business schools. Since in Britain the percentage of managers who have been through the business schools is so small, we cannot blame them. In industry, however, most people are employed initially as specialists, and often that specialism relies on 'rational' analysis, and career success is dependent on the ability to undertake that analysis effectively. In other words organisations value people who can operate in this way. Some managers continue to do what they have always done well, and use the methodologies which have served them well in the past. In the terms of Peters and Waterman, 'they are steeped in specialisation, standardisation, efficiency, productivity, and quantification, ... and run for cover when grubby operating decisions have to be made.' We are not usually told, but we suspect that the reason some of the managers end up on our courses is because they 'run for cover' when there are subordinates to be spoken to, or other managers to see, and they can no longer rely solely on the facts and the analysis.

DOING EVERYTHING 'BY THE BOOK'

Closely related to rationality is the influence of the culture in which we work. If you ask most people to describe the organisation in which they work, they draw the family tree or toasting fork to represent it. The assumption is that everything can and should be analysed in a logical fashion. This is the world of job descriptions and procedure manuals, budgets and information systems. This is the world of stability and predictability, where yesterday's experiences can be analysed and used as predictors for tomorrow, and the next day and the next day. In our heads we know that the world, for most of us, is not like that, although there are some organisations where it is fairly close to it. The strange thing is that managers will talk about being in 'fast-moving' consumer goods, or on the 'leading edge' of technology, but behave with people as if they are in a stable, predictable world. It is pleasant sometimes to be able to rely on the rules. It is far less taxing to look up the answer in the manual than to have to think the issue through yet again. It is certainly easier when dealing with people to be able to say, 'I'm sorry but the rules are clear on this matter ...', or to use the policy in order to avoid creating a precedent. This culture is secure psychologically, and indeed it often is contractually as well. It is not unusual for people in these cultures to believe that they will go on working there, perhaps for most of their working life. They may not say so, and they may even talk about moving, but if you look at career patterns, it is often true that people have been in the organisation for many years. The result of the culture, which is not very often recognised or made explicit, is that situations are handled in ways that are intended to avoid rocking the boat. Difficult problems are ignored or 'papered over'. Managers often behave as if they hoped things would improve given time, and of course they do not. Sometimes special departments are employed to deal with these irrational people problems – the recalcitrant is sent to personnel, or for some sorts of problem to see the nurse, often before the manager is really sure about the nature of the problem. In treating people as though their personality is an inconvenience, the manager will often behave as though he lost his when he was promoted.

THE DESIRE FOR CONTROL

Another feature of the 'rules and order' culture is the need to control everything. A manager's job can be seen as trying to keep things neat and tidy, and there is a sense of failure if the manager is not in control. Of course this is sometimes right, but there are many managerial situations with people, when this cannot be the case. It is probably true that some people have a greater need for control than others. This need is fostered by the belief that good managers are always in control, and if this is not so they should develop another system to ensure that they are next time. This will have a direct result on the way managers conduct interviews, particularly with subordinates. If a manager is disciplining someone, then to get them into the office, tell them what they have done, and what disciplinary action is being taken, keeping control of the interview at all times, is functional to achieving the purpose of that interview. However, if a subordinate comes to see his boss with a personal problem, and the boss is more concerned with keeping control than allowing the person to talk, they may never communicate effectively on the matter. It will not be surprising if the subordinate says to his workmates that the boss is not interested in helping, and gradually no one takes those kind of problems to that manager.

THE NEED FOR POWER

We think that recently there has been a strong movement towards macho management and an attraction to what Charles Handy, in his book *The Gods of Management*, calls the 'Zeus' culture, where the manager sends down his thunderbolts when he is angered, or showers gold when he is occasionally pleased. We have observed that looking good as a manager often means catching people doing things wrong, and putting them in their place. As Kenneth Blanchard and Spencer Johnson observed in *The One Minute Manager*, most managers store up bad behaviour, then tell people all the things they have done wrong for the last few weeks. Quite often you will hear a manager say that someone's performance is slipping, and if it goes on like this much longer 'I will have to say something to them!' Work review systems often collude with this tendency, and the manager feels that he will have nothing to say if he cannot hand out one or two thunderbolts, so they are stored up for the meeting. We think it is probably also true that in the British culture it is thought to be macho to tell people about their faults, and 'manly' to take your punishment and recognise your faults. What we are not very good at is recognising our strengths, and we, as British managers, are even worse at giving praise to people for things they have done well. It is as if the manager will lose status by saying 'Well done.' The result can be that whilst people want to be given recognition and would be motivated by that recognition, their main motivation becomes avoiding the punishment, or creating excuses so that they are not to blame. *The One Minute Manager* is an attempt to correct this imbalance, and offers some very positive strategies for certain types of interview with subordinates.

'DON'T TELL ME YOUR TROUBLES'

It is also our experience that even the kindest and most considerate managers, who would like to be able to help their subordinates, or even their colleagues, avoid doing so. They will often set up the interview that is supposed to help, and this may even be institutionalised, for example, in the pre-disciplinary counselling process. This is designed to give the subordinate the opportunity to improve, and therefore to avoid discipline. Most managers we have met would prefer to do this, and would be willing to try to help. However, in the interview itself the manager often fails to understand the problem, or deals with the symptom rather than the cause, and is then surprised when it recurs.

Sometimes this is related to the macho manager syndrome, where the belief is that it is more appropriate to listen and then tell the person what they must do than to get involved in personal problems. There is nothing wrong with this approach, although it is not as helpful as the system implies. More often though, the manager is more than willing to help. Questions will be asked, assistance given, to help the subordinate identify the problem. However, what we have observed many times is that just as the problem starts to be identified, the manager closes off the interview or diverts the discussion to a symptom. It is as if they feel that this is 'too personal' for me to handle, and that if I go any further I will not be able to cope with whatever emerges. Of course this may be the case in extreme problems, but more often the closing down occurs long before the manager is able to make that judgement. In any case, as we will discuss in Part 2 of the book, the manager is not called upon to be the expert and solve the problem, but to help the subordinate to think of solutions or ways of handling the consequences of the problem in terms of work.

Most managers are not trained to conduct interviews in work, or if they are this is only with regard to selection interviews. If we accept Rosemary Stewart's findings that the manager spends a large percentage of his time in one-to-one meetings, then it is in these interviews that help is needed. The great myth is that it comes naturally. Most of us have to learn from the way we have been treated in similar interviews, or by trial and error. Sometimes that can be a very costly way to learn, and the risk is that managers find a formula which has worked for them once, and they continue to use it for all circumstances, even though the people and perhaps the purpose have changed. We have worked with many a sales manager who treats every interview as though it were a sale. He tries to sell the subordinates everything from improving their performance, through accepting change, to redundancy. The results can be catastrophic. It is not just salesmen who do this. We know personnel managers who turn everything into a negotiation, and specialists who want to provide the answer even before they understand the problem.

Try completing this questionnaire about the time you spend interviewing, who you communicate with, what you find easy and what creates problems.

Which interviews do you handle well?

Which interviews do you find difficult?

What proportion of your time is spent interviewing? ....%

One of the key ways that you can think about interviews is 'With whom do they take place?' Try to indicate what percentage of your interviews would fall into the following categories:

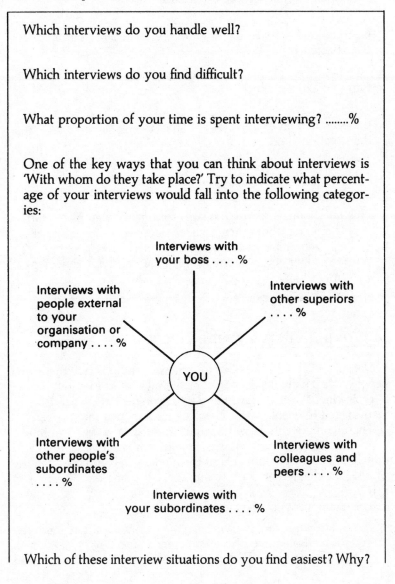

Which of these interview situations do you find easiest? Why?

Which of these situations do you find hardest? Why?

Link these answers back to the profile on reasons why you do interviews on page 3. As we have said, it is usual that people find some interviews easier than others, because they are more comfortable or have more experience.

Can you find an example of an interview where you did not feel effective?

Can you explain why?

Can you find an example of an interview where you handled the situation well?

Can you explain why?

This questionnaire is used in some of our workshops to start people thinking about their own learning needs. It is used here to help you think about your own interviewing expertise before reading the sections on planning, analysis and preparation.

Improving interview effectiveness

We often talk about the skilled interviewer, and it is true that some people have a natural ability to cope with the difficulties involved in interviewing. We shall now identify the components which have to be managed to enable you to become a competent interviewer.

These components have been put together in a practical model which enables managers to analyse and plan effective communications. Each of the components of the model will be discussed in the subsequent chapters in Part 1, and applied to specific situations in Part 2.

The components of the model are:

- Clarifying the purpose of the communication, and the desired outcome of the interview or meeting
- Understanding the aspects of the interview which can and

should be planned in advance, and those which will have to be managed as the meeting progresses

- Being in the appropriate role to achieve the purpose of the interview
- Understanding how the values, attitudes, needs and expectations of both people will influence the interview
- Understanding and managing the pressures and influences which are brought into the interview by both people
- Using the appropriate skills to achieve the desired outcome of the communication.

These components are brought together in a model of interviewing which looks like this:

An integrated model of effective interviewing

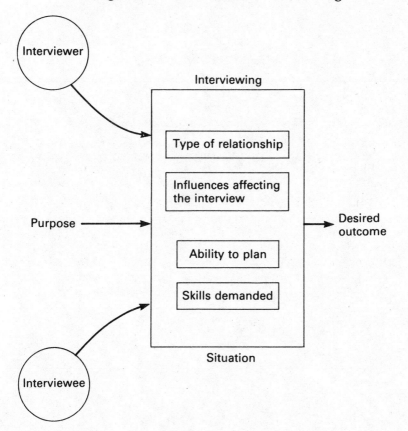

We have found that most people use their skill much more effectively if they have a plan which gives them some confidence, and if
that plan is based on a thorough analysis of the situation they are
trying to tackle. Of course the more experienced you become at
analysing the relevant factors, planning and carrying out interviews,
the more confident you become and the more you are able to use
your skill effectively. In the next chapters we will describe the
factors to be managed, give some practical examples, and build a
model which will help you to analyse and plan your interviews.

➤

CHAPTER TWO

Purposeful Communication

We know that the most powerful way of improving your communications is to be clear about *why* you are communicating. If you were a production manager you would not say, 'I think I will make some soap today.' You would want to be clear about the type of soap, the colour, the quantity, and many other things before you started. It is the same with interviews. Managers usually have a reason for interviewing someone, but that reason is often not defined clearly enough.

What is the purpose?

In many boss–subordinate interviews the purpose is to improve the performance of the subordinate. That could be true of a regular work review, an annual appraisal, a pre-disciplinary counselling session, a disciplinary interview, and so on. This very broad purpose is, therefore, not very helpful in giving a sense of direction to the interview. The boss needs to know exactly what is wanted for that particular interview. In regular work reviews the boss may have a very clear idea that he is trying to develop the skills or knowledge of a subordinate: he may be able to define what will make a skilled person, and even how long that learning will normally take. What the skilled boss will do, on the basis of knowledge about that subordinate's capabilities, is to set realistic outcomes for each interview.

We have, therefore, found it useful to distinguish between the larger, or longer-term *purpose*, and the often short-term but specific *outcome* for interviews. It is only by being clear about these that it is possible to judge the effectiveness of the interviews.

Without the purpose and outcome being clearly thought out, the interviewer may try to achieve more than is possible in one meeting and confuse the interviewee. We know from the many meetings that we overhear in hotel lobbies that a major problem some managers face is that they do not see their subordinates every day, indeed the meetings can be quite infrequent. We often listen to a regional sales manager telling a salesman about the latest promotions, monitoring the last month's figures, trying to motivate the salesman, giving him information about the company − and then, with that phrase we hear so often, 'And while you're here ...' adding on one more item. Just how much stays with the salesman? Certainly it is often very unclear which of the items the manager expected to be treated as priority. We are not arguing that these opportunities do not have to be taken and used to best advantage, but the good manager recognises that the 'interview' is being used to achieve several outcomes, and he uses devices which separate the parts and ensure that the other person knows which are the most important items.

THE PURPOSE OF AN EXIT INTERVIEW

The interview is between the personnel officer and John Rowlands, who has written a letter resigning from his job as storeman in the spares department of a large car distributors.

Personnel Officer: Thank you for coming to see me John. I need to be sure that you have all the papers that you need before you leave tomorrow, but I also wanted to have a chat with you about why you're leaving. You've been with us now for about five months and have decided to leave. You said in your resignation letter that you've got a better job. What does that mean?

John: Well it's more money, and it's not such a big place.

PO: Why do you want to work in a smaller company?

John: It'll be easier to get to know the other people and I'll get more chance to talk to the customers.

PO: What was your experience of talking to the customers here?

John: Well I got onto the counter occasionally, but most of the time I was finding things for the orders and that gets boring.

PO: What would have made it more interesting?

John: Well I don't mind being in the stores, but I only got to go on the counter when there was no one else around, like at dinner time, and you know how busy it can be then.

PO: I'm sure that you know it's company policy for you to work in the stores for the first few months, so that you get to know all the parts before you work on the counter. You knew this when you came, so what made you decide to leave?

John: Well some people always get stuck in the stores. The supervisor has his favourites and lets them work on the counter. Anyway he has his way of doing things and he doesn't want any new ideas.

PO: Did you suggest other ways of doing things?

John: Yes.

PO: How did you go about suggesting it?

John: I know what you're saying. You think I opened my mouth before I'd been there five minutes ...

PO: Well sometimes we can be too enthusiastic. What happened?

John: Well I told Mr Moxon that the new Renault spares department has this great way that the customer can find the part number themselves. I said 'Why couldn't we do that?' He said it wouldn't be worth the bother, and the way we do things now is perfectly all right. I didn't get on the counter again.

PO: Do you think you were a bit hasty in suggesting changes?

John: Maybe, but I don't think he'd ever want my ideas.

PO: Well I hope you get more opportunity to use your ideas in your new job. Is there anything else you want to tell me?

John: No, I don't think so.

PO: Well let me take this opportunity to wish you luck in your new job, and thank you for coming to see me.

*   *   *

What is the desired outcome from this interview?

- to find out why John is leaving?
- to find out about the supervision in the stores?
- to try to stop John leaving?
- to ensure that John leaves feeling positive about the company?
- to give John some idea of why the job has not worked for him?

- to make sure he does not think that it is the company's fault?
- to give John some career counselling?

The purpose of the interview is not clear. The earlier questions from the personnel officer suggest that it is to find out why John is leaving, but the statement about the company policy is more to do with letting him know that his expectations were unrealistic. It then moves into a phase of 'career counselling' to suggest that he learns from his experience. It finishes with an attempt to give him a positive impression of the company.

It would not be surprising if John were confused about why he was asked to come for the interview. The problem is not that the personnel officer is unskilled, but more likely that 'exit interviews' are a routine, and that the desired outcome for this interview has not been clarified.

———————————▶

Trying to achieve too complex an outcome in one interview is to risk confusing the other person. It is our experience that the more straightforward the desired outcome the more chance there is that it will be achieved.

How to end an interview

Another important thing about having a clear understanding of the outcome that you are trying to achieve is that it helps you to know when to finish the interview. So often we are asked to help people who want to know when and how to finish interviews. The most helpful advice we can give is to be sure what you are trying to achieve. Once you have achieved it – *stop*. If you go on after that you may bring in another topic which dilutes the impact of the main point you were trying to make, and at worst you may dig yourself a hole which will undo what you have achieved.

This is often what happens in the tough interviews – disciplinary ones for example. Managers may feel uncomfortable about having to discipline a subordinate, but they know that it has to be done. The interview may go perfectly well. The manager keeps control, tells the subordinate what he has done wrong, for example been late so many times, and that as a result he will have a formal record on

his file of the consequent warning. So far so good. It would probably be best to check with the subordinate that he understands and
then finish the interview. In fact, the experienced manager knows
that this kind of formal disciplinary interview will normally be quite
short. The less experienced manager feels uncomfortable with the
whole thing and will often invite the subordinate for his comments.
There follows a discussion about the rights and wrongs of the
situation. It quickly becomes confused as to whether this is a
disciplinary interview or a pre-disciplinary counselling session. It is
then not surprising if the subordinate is unsure whether he has been
disciplined or not.

────▶ EXAMPLES OF PURPOSES AND OUTCOMES

The disciplinary interview

Usually the *purpose* of disciplinary interviews and of the whole
disciplinary process, is to improve people's work performance.
Once the discussions and counselling have occurred, the
supervisor or manager needs to establish in the formal interview that the subordinate understands that disciplinary action
has been taken, and what it is. That is the required *outcome*
from a successful disciplinary interview.

The work review interview

The *purpose* of this interview could well be the same as the
disciplinary interview − to improve work performance. The
desired *outcome* from a specific interview will, of course, be
very different and will vary with the circumstances and the
subordinate concerned. The *outcome* could be that the subordinate understands that you are very pleased with his work. It
could be that he identifies areas of the job that need to be
strengthened or that require extra resources. It could be that
together you agree a plan of action to overcome some difficulty, or it could be very specific, for example that he accepts a
particular means of increasing sales which you specify.

The career counselling interview

The *purpose* of this interview is usually to help the individual develop plans and activities to assist with his career, and the interviewer will have to identify a sensible *outcome* for each interview. In this counselling role it will be necessary to find out where the interviewee is in his thinking. He may simply feel uneasy with his current job, and the outcome of the interview is that he identifies the nature of the problem in relation to his career. He may be clear about the problem and the *outcome* is that he identifies the possible courses of action which are open to him. If these things are clear, the *outcome* may be that a choice is made, and that plans are made. If they are not clear, a sensible *outcome* may be that a source of information is identified, and an agreement to meet again is made. All of these may be sensible *outcomes* depending on the person concerned, but if the counsellor starts to provide information, or tries to agree a plan of action before the interviewee is clear about the nature of the problem, the *outcome* will not be achieved. What is also clear from this example is that the achievement of the overall purpose may take several interviews, and indeed some people will need time between each stage to consolidate their thinking, while others will be able to move from one stage to the other in one interview.

Specialist interview with line manager

The *purpose* of many of the interviews between a management services specialist, for example, and the company's line managers will probably be to monitor or improve the productivity in that department. The *outcome* for a specific interview could be, for example, to inform the manager about his current costs, or the results of a recent study of some part of his departmental work. The management services consultant may decide, knowing his line manager, that simply informing him is never enough and that it would be sensible to go further than just giving the results, and to press for an agreed plan of action.

Is the outcome always clear?

With some interviews, like the disciplinary, or even more the termination or redundancy interview, the outcome that is required for the interview to be successful is very clear. In others, for example career counselling or a personal/domestic problem, the interviewer or counsellor may have no clear idea of a sensible outcome before the interview starts. Part of the task will be to formulate, and often negotiate with the interviewee an acceptable outcome.

What if aims conflict?

It is normal for the other person at an interview to have a quite different purpose, or different understanding of the purpose, and therefore to be aiming for a different outcome. Often a first step in successful interviewing is to ensure that both parties agree or accept the purpose and the outcome they are trying to achieve.

In some interviews you must accept that the other person will be trying to achieve a different outcome from you. In a disciplinary interview it would be quite normal for the subordinate to try to stop you achieving the outcome you want. As one manager on a course wrote about an unsuccessful interview, 'I was trying to reprimand a subordinate for her work output, and she kept bringing up all sorts of things that were not relevant, and getting away from the point.' Another wrote, 'I just wanted to tell them about the changes that would take place the following month, but they insisted on talking about the reason for and validity of the decision. At the end of the interview I did not feel that I had covered all the points I wanted to, and had certainly not presented them in the way I had planned.'

In both of these examples the interviewee had used a strategy of pursuing another outcome as a means of ensuring that the boss does not achieve his. This is sometimes a conscious strategy, but it is our experience that it happens quite spontaneously when people feel strongly about the outcome. After all, how often do you hear a mother say to quite young children 'Will you listen and stop changing the subject!'

In other cases the interviewee may misunderstand the purpose, perhaps because they are carrying a preconception based on previous experience. People learn from their experiences and often that experience leads them to misinterpret what is said to them. This is called selective perception, and it means that the person only hears those things which fit their expectations. For example, the boss can say, 'If you have any problems, please let me know', but the subordinate may have a lot of previous experience that says people in authority only complain if you get things wrong. The boss can then set up an interview to review work, and be quite prepared to help the subordinate with problems, only to find that there are none, or none that the subordinate is prepared to admit. He may see the purpose of the interview as explaining performance in terms of outside influences, rather than reviewing personal difficulties.

Another example, of which we have considerable experience, is the appraisal interview. We are often asked to help companies to improve or install a new appraisal scheme. Of course most people have experience of being appraised, and that often means 'being told by the boss what he thinks of you'. Many of the newer schemes are intended as a joint problem-solving session where both parties are looking for ways of improving performance. This can be explained at meetings and in writing, although many staff still behave at the appraisal interview as if expecting the boss to tell them what he thinks. They then come out of the interview convinced that nothing has changed in spite of the boss's good intentions. It often means that the manager has to work hard at clarifying the purpose of the interview, actively checking with the interviewee that it is understood, and looking for signs during the interview that the purpose is really accepted.

In the following case study we have illustrated the importance of purpose and outcome in a typical communication announcing an unpopular change.

————▶

WHAT OUTCOME WOULD YOU AIM FOR HERE?

The policy change interview

As part of a cost-cutting and efficiency exercise the management has taken the decision to form typing/secretarial pools in the company and to do away with individual secretaries for the middle management.

You are the senior manager of a department in which each of three middle managers working for you has his own secretary. Next month the three women who work for your managers will go to a 'pool', initially to share the new word processor and continue to do the work of the managers, but eventually to provide a joint secretarial/administrative service for the whole department. You as the senior manager will retain your own secretary. Your managers will have to decide how they want their filing done and so on. For example, they may keep it in their own office or have the women continuing to do it in the general office. The secretaries will still receive incoming telephone calls, but the outgoing calls will be dialled by the manager himself.

In addition to economy, it is hoped that the new methods will make better use and control of new and existing equipment like the word processors and photocopiers. It should also smooth out the peaks and troughs in demand for secretarial services and avoid the situation of some secretaries working overtime, when others are underloaded.

You are going to explain the changes to your managers. You have decided to see them separately and to start with Harry Hind, who you think is the most likely to be upset by the change.

WHAT IS YOUR OVERALL PURPOSE? WHAT ARE YOUR OUTCOME CHOICES?

Given that the decision has already been made, the overall purpose is to ensure that the new set-up works, preferably with the co-operation of everyone concerned. If the decision had not been made, there would be options about how far the staff should be consulted, and on which issues they should, or should not, be consulted. As the senior manager in this case you have no choice but to make it work. The real choices are in the possible outcomes from this particular interview:

- That Harry will leave the interview convinced of the appropriateness of the new arrangement. This is the ex-salesman's outcome. He would believe that he could sell Harry the benefits of it. The manager who relies heavily on rationality might also choose this outcome, convincing himself that the facts speak for themselves, and he would be surprised if Harry objected.
- That Harry will accept the changes and work willingly to make them succeed. This would be very nice, and make it easy for the manager, but it does not account for the fact that most people do not like having their personal secretary taken away.
- That you will tell Harry what the changes are, and send him away to come back with proposals about making the new arrangement work. This is quite a sensible outcome, and managers who like to keep things under tight control are likely to be attracted to

it. It ignores the fact that Harry is likely to be quite upset about the changes and will probably need an opportunity to voice his objections.

- That you will tell Harry what the changes are, give him the opportunity to voice his concerns, but still get him working positively on how to overcome the difficulties which may arise from the new arrangements. This may provide the best outcome for Harry. There is no point in debating the 'rights and wrongs' of the decision, so telling him is appropriate, but since most people would feel upset if they were subjected to such a major change in their working pattern, they will almost certainly want the opportunity to tell you what is wrong with the decision. They need to 'get it off their chest', and having done so will usually begin to work positively, if that is what you direct them to do.

These are not the only possible outcomes, indeed in the training situation we have seen the interview end either in a row, or the senior manager going back to his bosses to see if the decision can be renegotiated! These obviously are not satisfactory outcomes. The successful interviewer will consider a number of alternatives to decide which is the most appropriate in their own circumstances, with the particular person concerned, and given the overall purpose that they want to achieve.

$\longrightarrow$

CHAPTER THREE

Planning Communication

It is useful to think of interviews in terms of their ability to be planned in advance – their 'planability'. Some interviews can and should be planned beforehand. For example, the formal warning which is part of the disciplinary procedure should be planned to such an extent that the 'script' for it is often written in advance and approved by the personnel officer.

At the other end of the spectrum there are interviews which cannot be planned at all. When someone comes to you with a personal problem, you cannot predetermine the outcome, let alone what will be said, or what issues you will have to deal with.

The extent to which an interview can be planned will often help you to determine the appropriate role, the skills you will need to use, and may also suggest a structure for the interview.

What determines how far interviews can be planned?

IS THE REQUIRED OUTCOME KNOWN?

We have already discussed this in Chapter 2, but the guideline is: the more the outcome is known and considered necessary for the success of the interview, the more it can be planned.

In the tough managerial interviews like disciplinary terminations and those announcing redundancy, the required outcome is very clear in advance. If it is not clear, then you are dealing with some other kind of interview.

This is not only true in managerial interviews, but in many fact-finding interviews, for example those carried out by a management services specialist. Certain questions must be asked and certain topics covered, otherwise the interviewer will not be able to under-take the analysis which they have designed.

ARE THERE PROCEDURES YOU MUST FOLLOW?

We have already mentioned the example of the disciplinary interview, and the same is true of a termination interview, where it is
necessary to say certain things and to check that they are understood, so that the legal requirements of the interview are met. Some
companies have a procedure for handling grievances. This is partly
to ensure that the employee has a reasonable method of making his
complaint known, but it is also for the protection of the manager.

Some interviews do not follow a procedure in that sense, but it is
necessary to cover certain topics, often in an agreed way. Much
time is devoted to training managers to conduct appraisal interviews, and here it is essential to cover specified topics or it will not
be possible to complete the form at the end of the interview. This
does not imply that an appraisal form should determine the
sequence of the topics discussed, although some managers do use
the form as a set procedure, following it slavishly. It is an interview
that is partly prescribed by the appraisal procedure of the company,
and it could be quite different in another organisation. Some parts of
it can normally be pre-planned.

HAVE YOU DONE YOUR HOMEWORK?

The outcome that you are aiming for in some interviews necessit-
ates that you know all the relevant facts before you begin. You
would be very unwise to start an interview which is accusing
someone of not having completed a piece of work by an agreed
time, if it is likely to degenerate into an argument about whether it
was completed or not. You would be even more unwise to start a
disciplinary interview accusing someone of stealing, unless you
were absolutely confident about your facts. If the required outcome
is that you will inform someone, then you should be the one who
knows the facts, and can predetermine what the content of the
interview will be.

In other cases the interviewee is the one who has the facts and
can determine the content of the interview. In the early stages of a
career counselling session, the content and the facts to be discussed
are those brought in by the interviewee. For the interviewer the
extent to which it can be planned may be very limited, especially if
it is someone that they do not know well.

CONTROLLING THE INTERVIEW

We talked earlier about the need that some people have to control interviews, but the desired outcome will often determine the need for control. Sometimes there is a need to control the content of what is discussed or brought into the interview, and at others the control is obtained through the structure, and particularly the sequence in which things are brought into the interview.

The interviewer will often obtain control, and appropriately so, by specifying the purpose of the meeting, and by stating what can be talked about and what is not relevant to the meeting. In the interview with Harry Hind in Chapter 2, the manager might well state the purpose of the meeting, and add that there is no point in discussing the rights or wrongs of the decision, since there is nothing that either of them can do about it. In this way he is able to control the content of the interview. In an interview to terminate someone's employment the same thing would be appropriate. The manager might well start with a statement of the purpose, continue with the reasons for the dismissal, and only allow the subordinate to ask questions to check understanding. This ensures that the case is not opened up for discussion again, after the decision has been made. In fact, in both these cases it will be in the interviewee's interest to discuss the decision in the hope that it can be changed. If the manager allows the interview to go that way, it is possible that the outcome will either not be achieved at all, or only achieved at some cost. Planning and sticking to the plan are essential.

The other means of control is to set a structure for the interview, deciding the sequence of the topics to be raised, and determining how each part will be handled.

AN EXAMPLE OF CONTROL, USING STRUCTURE

The manager wants to announce a change in working practice, which is not likely to be popular. It can be structured so that discussion is allowed on the parts where it may be helpful to the outcome, and not on others. It could be structured like this:

> Statement of purpose
> 'I have asked you to come and see me today to tell you about the changes that will come into force next month ...'
>
> Statement of facts or the case for the changes, and then the facts, summarising on the key issues, and the actions that have to be taken.

Invitation of questions to clarify understanding, reinforcing that the decision is not open for discussion. (It must be expected that if the decision is unpopular there will normally be a mixture of questions to clarify understanding, views about the decision, complaints, criticism about the management, and doubts about its viability.)

The control is maintained by the manager staying within the structure. Only questions for clarification would be picked up, answered, and the summary repeated. By listening to the other points but not arguing, the control can be maintained.

Of course it may not feel that easy when you are doing it, but the structure does provide a means of control because the interviewer can keep returning to it. If he is tempted to go outside the structure, this would not be consistent with the desired outcome. It is our experience that many managers like a good argument, and happily pick up the irrelevant points, but this does not lead to effective interviewing. Do not forget, it is usually quite consistent with the interviewee's desired outcome to get you to argue, because it seduces the manager away from the purpose! Plan the structure, and use it.

───────────────►

SUMMARY

An important factor for analysing and understanding interviews is to decide where a particular interview lies on a spectrum from those which can be planned in detail to those which cannot be planned at all. This will help you decide how far you should plan it, how much you need to check the facts beforehand, the amount of control that it is appropriate for you to have, and how much you should let the other person retain.

Highly 'planable' interviews:

- The facts and content are known
- The control is simpler, and usually with the interviewer
- It is clear what type of relationship is needed
- The use of interviewing skills is simpler
- There may be a procedure which prescribes the discussion.

Interviews which are low in 'planability':

- The facts and content may be unclear, or even unknown

- The control of the interview may be shared
- There is often a choice about the type of relationship which it is appropriate to build during the interview
- The use of interviewing skills is correspondingly more complex.

These last two points, the type of relationship and the skills used, will be the subject of the next two chapters.

▶

CHAPTER FOUR

The Right Role for the Job

Having decided what outcome you are aiming for, and to what extent the interview is prescribed, it will probably be clear what role you should be in, or what kind of relationship you will have to build during the interview. If it is a boss—subordinate interview there are a number of roles which you can adopt which are appropriate to achieving specific outcomes. These include being:

> Executive
> Adviser
> Tutor
> Consultant
> Counsellor.

But if you include the manager's relationships with other people, the list also includes planner, policy-maker, expert, auditor of standards, arbitrator, exemplar, representative of the group, scapegoat, friend, and probably quite a lot more.

We are very used to switching from one role to another in our social and family lives. In the family a man can move within the day from being husband, financial planner, father, friend, adviser, gardener, driver, and lover. As long as he is in the appropriate role for the task he is doing, this does not cause any difficulties for either his wife or his children. It is our experience that if we are in the wrong role, our children are very quick to remind us! In a particular situation you carry a 'set' of roles in relation to a number of people.

▶

YOUR WORKING ROLE SET

Think of a reasonably complex work situation and draw up **a role set** for yourself.

When you have drawn up the 'set', go round it and identify the role that you are normally expected to carry in relation to the other person or group. For example, you might be

This diagram represents the 'set' of roles that a man might have in his family situation

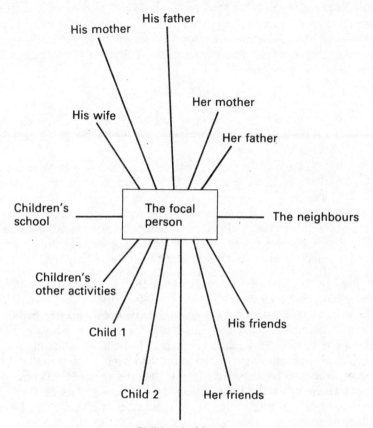

His father

His mother

Her mother

His wife

Her father

Children's school — The focal person — The neighbours

Children's other activities

His friends

Child 1

Child 2   Her friends

Children's friends

expected to be the expert adviser, the arbitrator, the representative of your own group, the subordinate to your boss, the planner or the standard setter.

We have found that most managers are surprised at the number of roles that they are regularly expected to play at work. In general, we move from one to the other quite naturally, and just as with the children in the family setting, we are quickly told when we are in a role which others feel is not appropriate: 'I don't think it's your job to plan for our department' or 'You can speak for your own group, but you don't have any right to speak for the rest of us!'

We know that sometimes at work people suffer from the indigestion of having too many roles to carry, and this is called *role overload*. At other times the roles that have to be played are in conflict with one another, or at the extremes incompatible. This can lead to what is called *role stress*. We do not intend to deal with role theory here, although it is well worth reading one of the good management books on the subject.

Our reasons for discussing a little of the theory are:

- it is important in planning your interviews that you decide on the role which is most appropriate for the outcome you want to achieve;
- you need to recognise that selecting the role is something that you practise in many ways at work, and in your social life;
- it is something that managers frequently get wrong because of the managerial culture in which they operate, the need for control or the need for power, or because they carry inappropriate role behaviour from other situations.

If the requirement of the interview is that a subordinate is told something that they must do, then the boss must be the boss, or in the executive role. On the other hand if the boss wants to explore what is going on, what the causes are, for example, of a drop in productivity, then it would be necessary to be in an enquiring role, such as consultant. Once the enquiries had been made it might still be necessary to be executive. In this case the required outcome of the interview would have changed from being fact-finding to decision-making and, therefore, it would be appropriate to have changed roles.

The **executive role** is not only appropriate in boss–subordinate interviews. It is also appropriate for the specialist when they have the authority to correct something, to change it, or to enforce approved standards. For example, the accountant who feels that certain practices are likely to endanger the security of the company's money, the personnel officer who believes that actions are contrary to the company's employment policy, or the lawyer who knows that something is against the law, should behave executively, even with staff who are senior to them in the company hierarchy.

If you do not have the authority to do something, perhaps the best outcome you can expect is that the other person will listen to your advice, based on your recognised expertise, and act on it. In that case the **advisory role** is appropriate. As the expert, if you really are, your advice can be very strong: 'You can make that decision, but if you don't take my advice the consequences will be …' The adviser can try to persuade, by the strength of argument, to sell the benefits, or if used to relying on rationality, simply to ensure that the other person knows the relevant facts. In many boss–subordinate interviews the boss would like to be the adviser, and 'hopes' that the subordinate will take the good advice, but of course the expertise is not always accepted, especially if it concerns their personal life or career.

If the outcome of an interview is that the other person will have learned something, then it is appropriate for the boss, or the specialist, to adopt a teaching or **tutorial role**. Very often it will be clear that a person's performance could be improved by increasing his knowledge, or the specialist may be asked to help someone, for example to use a particular computer package. In these cases the tutorial role is appropriate. This will involve thinking about what the person already knows, and taking them to the new level of knowledge, often working carefully to ensure that the learning is proceeding at the pace of the other person, not at the level of interest to the 'tutor'.

Sometimes the interviewee is coming to the interviewer to obtain some help with a problem related to work. This is often a major role for a manager. Subordinates are experts in their own area of work, but the boss is still asked to help them solve problems. This means that the subordinate wants them to be in a **consultative role**. The boss may want to work with the subordinate in a consultative way, rather than simply be the expert, so that the subordinate learns to solve that kind of problem for himself.

On other occasions it is the only way that the boss can work with the other person, because they have all the facts or information about the problem, and by the nature of the situation this cannot be altered without affecting the work. In a social-work setting the team manager cannot sit in on the work with clients without changing the relationship. The supervision is, therefore, usually of a consultative nature, with the manager helping the social worker to think through the problems for himself. Of course in industry and commerce we are used to the word 'consultant' meaning expert, but it is now becoming much more popular for experts or specialists to work in a consultative role to ensure that the solution is something that the 'client' manager can use, and that really fits his problem.

Close to this but more relevant to personal problems is the **counselling role**. This is usually applied in situations where a boss is trying to help the subordinate with career issues, personal or domestic problems, or work problems that arise because of some personal difficulty. The reason why it is appropriate to work from a counselling role, which means working from where the person is, and helping him solve the problem in ways which are suited to him, is that the individual has to implement the solution with his own skills, abilities and emotions, and not with the boss's. Of course this way of working is a role which is often demanded of the personnel officer, or the industrial nurse, but in many organisations it is an important role for the manager to be able to play as well. We believe that this is particularly important and have devoted a chapter in Part 2 to the subject of the manager and counselling.

CHANGING ROLES AS THE INTERVIEW DEVELOPS

In a grievance interview when the person bursts through the door, or stops you in the corridor, you may have no idea what they want. It would be very sensible to take on the role of fact-finder first, only becoming an adviser when you understand the problem and can decide on your first desired outcome. If that does not work you may have to switch to executive and tell them what they must do. The important thing is that this changing role is conscious. Remember that the interviewee may have another purpose, and one of the most common ways of putting the interviewer off their stride is to seduce them into another role. The subordinate you want to discipline may well try to seduce you out of the executive role into the advisory 'Well what would you do about it?', and then into the friend role 'We've worked together for five years ...'

In cross-functional interviews you may have decided that the appropriate role is advisory, or even consultative, but it is not unusual for the person you are trying to advise to try to manœuvre you into the executive role, so that you are responsible for the outcome. If you do change your role, you need to be aware of it, and be sure that it still fits with the outcome you are trying to achieve.

EXAMPLES OF ROLE, PURPOSE AND OUTCOME

The disciplinary interview

In the early stages of the disciplinary process different roles may be necessary, for example fact-finder, adviser, counsellor, friend, but once the decision has been made to discipline a subordinate formally it is unlikely that this will be successfully achieved with any role other than executive. This is a highly prescribed interview, and it is clear that this is the appropriate relationship. If you take your subordinate to the pub and try to do it as a friend, do not be surprised if they fail to realise that they have been disciplined.

The redundancy interview

The process of making someone redundant often has many stages. These may include the announcement of the fact, telling them about the conditions of the redundancy, and then providing various kinds of help and support. Obviously each of these stages has different required outcomes, and it is our experience that it is often best to separate the stages into different interviews to avoid confusion. If we think about the first of these, telling someone that they are going to be made redundant, the role which best fits the task and the desired outcome is executive. Any other role would risk confusing the message, but it also has another purpose and that is to protect the feelings of the manager announcing the redundancy. It is best done as a formal interview, and with the boss in the formal executive role. Again it is highly prescribed, and the control is with the interviewer when they are in the executive role, which helps to ensure that the outcome is achieved. This will feel very uncomfortable for many people. Since most of us do not like conducting redundancy interviews, it is very easy to slip out of the executive role into information-giver, adviser, or even salesman selling the advantages of redundancy. In our experience even if this does not create confusion, it often leads to argument and leaves a bad taste not only about the redundancy, but also about the way it was handled.

The interview with personnel

Very often the ordinary employee does not have much to do with the personnel department except on formal occasions, and tends to see the personnel officer as the provider of information on what to do about sickness or pensions or something similar. If then the manager arranges for the same employee to see personnel about a personal matter, they may well expect them to have a similar role – 'expert adviser on personal matters'. The personnel officer has been trained that the best way to work with people on personal problems is in the counselling role, trying to help the employee think through the problem, identify their options, and commit themselves to a particular course of action. All the time the employee is waiting for the magic advice which never comes, and may leave the interview saying, 'It was a complete waste of time. All they did was ask questions.' The personnel officer chose a role which they felt was appropriate for the desired outcome, but because the employee expected another role, there was some confusion. Often it is necessary to explain the role you are taking and get it accepted by the other person, so that you can work effectively together.

Do not confuse role with style

Each of us has our own style of talking and working with people and, therefore, of conducting interviews. Our natural style can be formal or assertive and the executive role may fit easily with that style. If your style is more relaxed or even tentative, the interviews demanding an executive role may feel more difficult. It does not mean you have to be noisy and have two telephones on your desk to be executive. A quiet, even gentle, but firm style can be just as effective. Clarity about the role, and conducting the interview within your own style, is likely to be more effective than copying someone else's style.

The implication of this is that some styles fit some roles more easily than others. If you tend to listen carefully before you speak, the career counselling, consultative, or fact-finding roles may come easily to you. If you are quick, decisive and do not find it difficult to say 'No', the executive interviews will fit better with your style. In either case you will have to work harder at some interviews than others, but the role relates to the job you are doing, or the outcome, and clarity about that will help you achieve it with your own style.

Is role-playing a pose?

A question that often comes up on our courses is: 'Does playing a role mean I'm acting? Won't people see through that?' At one level, as we have pointed out, 'playing' different roles is very natural, and even playing several at the same time is something which we learn to do from childhood. Yet the idea seems to be difficult, and it can lead to difficulties in interviews.

From the interviewer's point of view the problem seems to be either that there is a feeling of falseness about behaving differently, or that 'you should always be yourself'. We would not disagree with people being themselves in interviews. Indeed on our courses we work hard to help people understand that they must use their own skills and abilities, and not try to copy other people because that will certainly be seen as false. What we also know is that 'false' behaviour is very quickly sensed by the other person. They may not be able to articulate the reason, but they will often say, 'Well I wouldn't trust them.'

----▶

DIFFERENT PERCEPTIONS

This is a problem which has been tackled not only by psychologists, but also by philosophers, and to quote one of them, Martin Buber:

> Imagine two men, whose life is dominated by appearances, sitting and talking together. Call them Peter and Paul. Let us list the different configurations which are involved. First there is Peter as he wishes to appear to Paul and Paul as he wishes to appear to Peter. Then there is Peter as he really appears to Paul, that is, Paul's image of Peter, which in general does not in the least coincide with what Peter wishes Paul to see; and similarly there is the reverse situation. Further there is Peter as he appears to himself, and Paul as he appears to himself. Lastly, there are the bodily Peter and the bodily Paul, two living beings and six ghostly appearances, which mingle in many ways in the conversation between the two. Where is there room for any genuine inter-human life?

----▶

The problem is an analytical one, not a practical one. Indeed the quantity of information which can be thrown up from this kind of analysis can be paralysing. Action can seem quite impossible in the face of all that data. It also seems, however, that normal socialisation, the process of growing and learning, gives us the ability to make, and express, the necessary discriminations. In work we relate to each other on the basis of roles, and we know that different people would perform those roles differently. We therefore acknowledge that behind the role relationships are people and personalities.

This must affect the interview. In work we get to know people very well, and can allow for and work with the 'people' as well as the jobs they have to do.

Reproduced courtesy of *The Evening Standard*

In everyday life that makes us prefer to deal with one cashier rather than another at the bank, it means that we check if the boss is in a good mood before we ask for certain things, or we take the opportunity of getting something changed with one supervisor, because we know that another would want all the forms completed in triplicate!

From this kind of analysis we have developed a simple model which has been helpful to people conducting interviews. People relate to each other in their roles, and those roles imply values, attitudes, needs and expectations. Knowing those roles and when they are in conflict can be helpful in planning the interview.

A simple work example might be if you as a manager want to get something from the stores, and you know that the chief storekeeper insists on having all the paperwork completed accurately. You might get away with using your authority, but it would be more effective to ensure that you have the forms completed. The 'interview' would be much quicker, since you would be meeting his job needs, and you would not risk the argument which might follow and which would almost certainly affect your long-term relationship with him..

Check

- That the role you are in fits the outcome you want to achieve;
- That the other person's expectations of your role are not different from yours;
- That you are not being seduced into an inappropriate role;
- That you do not confuse role and style.

CHAPTER FIVE

Values, Attitudes, Needs and Expectations

It is helpful to consider the ways in which values, attitudes, needs and expectations affect communications. You may feel as a boss that you should have an open, friendly way of working with people, and that if subordinates have problems they should come and tell you. And yet how often do you hear a manager say, 'Why on earth didn't you tell me about this before?' The subordinate may well have expectations that bosses are not interested in personal problems, or that they are much too busy with major problems to be concerned with 'my little problems'. You may feel that as the boss you should keep a sensible distance from the people who work for you, and yet this may be seen as cold and remote. This is to attribute personal characteristics from the role behaviour. They are related, but for analytical, and planning purposes we have separated them.

Not only do the values, attitudes, needs and expectations of each party affect the role relationship, but they also affect the personal relationship. The boss and the subordinate will carry values and attitudes, as people, and about other people, into interviews, and this will affect the way they are conducted. For example, a boss may have been instructed not to pass information on to his staff, but since he holds values about honesty in personal relationships this can be very difficult. A subordinate may want to tell their boss about some personal difficulties, but since the boss believes that people should be allowed to keep personal things to themselves, he or she may, unconsciously, prevent the person from telling them about their troubles.

However, the personal values and expectations can also be used to overcome problems in role relationships. A subordinate may feel that he would not normally talk to a boss about this kind of problem, but in the case of this particular boss, he has learned to trust him as a person and will be able to confide in him. Many cross-functional difficulties are overcome by these personal relationships:

'I don't usually expect accountants to be interested in or to understand what we are doing in our department, but if you go to see
Elizabeth you will find her very helpful.'

One of the keys to successful interviewing is to use an approach
which fits the values of the other person, and this is the advantage
of getting to know the people with whom you work, and not
assuming that they all hold the same values as you.

VALUES, ATTITUDES AND NEEDS: THE MANAGER

You are the manager of the Management Services Department. Your department is going to be transferred in six
months time to another site some 160 miles away, close to the
warehouse in Leicester. You are going to move and will
continue to manage your department. You are trying to
persuade the other members of the department to move with
you, particularly those in key jobs.

One of these is Jim Eaton, a very competent project
manager, who is leading one of your most important projects,
the introduction of a new direct ordering system. He is not
indispensable, but it would have very serious consequences for
the project if he left. You need him for another year, at almost
any price.

He is 30 years old, married, with three children, one of
whom he has expressed some concern about from time to time
for health reasons. If he did not move, he would find it difficult
in the current economic climate to get a job in the area with
similar interest and a similar salary.

You do not know whether or not he will be prepared to
move, but you have to consider how to conduct an interview
with him in either case.

The purpose of this interview

The best long-term purpose for this interview is that Jim decides to
move to Leicester. Since he is so valuable to the project, perhaps the
next best purpose is that at least you retain him, in some way, for
another year. If neither of these is possible, a third would be that
you find out as soon as you can, so that you put yourself in a good
position to replace him quickly. You will also need to do it in a way
that retains his good will, so that the work on the project continues

with as little disturbance as possible. You are unlikely to achieve any of these in one interview, but the outcome from the interview needs to be consistent with your chosen purpose. As it happens these purposes provide reasonable fall-back positions, and it is often helpful to have these in this kind of interview.

The required outcome

The minimum you need to achieve is that Jim knows that the move is going to take place in six months time, and that you will need to know fairly quickly if he will be coming with you. You will probably need to ensure that he knows how valuable he is to the project, and that you really want him to complete his work on it.

If you achieve this, you might ask him to talk with his wife, and arrange a meeting so that you can discuss the inevitable problems and ways to overcome them.

An alternative would be to ensure that he knows about the move, and to find out what his attitude is and what problems would need to be overcome to enable him to move to Leicester.

Another alternative would be to try to persuade him to move with you to Leicester, by helping him to overcome any difficulties he might have.

Another outcome might be that you tell him about the move, find out if he is willing to come with you, and, if not, tell him that he should look for another job since he will be replaced as soon as possible.

To some extent the alternative you choose may be determined by the values and expectations you hold, either as a manager or as a person, about how people should feel about their jobs. We have certainly worked with people who feel that they and their company should do everything possible to help Jim move, and others who have a much more 'take it or leave it' approach and feel that the responsibility for the decision is with the individual. Some may feel that it is their duty to try to persuade Jim to move, but if there is any resistance, that is his problem and not theirs. The values you hold, partly as a person, and partly in the role of manager, will influence the way you choose to tackle the interview. It is therefore worth generating a list of alternative outcomes, and considering if your preferred choice is consistent with the task you have to do or more a reflection of your values.

If you decide to try and persuade him to move as part of this interview, what arguments will you use? It is not unusual for people to try some combination of the following:

- He is important to the project, and they are quite sure that he wouldn't like to leave it unfinished.
- For the success of the project it is important to keep the team together.
- There will be many advantages to living near Leicester, especially since the housing will be much cheaper, and it will lead to a much higher standard of living.
- The company will of course pay all the removal costs, and there will be an allowance to help people settle in. Hotel and travelling costs will be paid, if there is a gap between moving and finding a suitable house.
- Although you know there are some health problems with one of the children, there are very good hospitals in Leicester, and the company doctor is available to liaise with the hospital there.
- It will be very difficult to get another comparable job in the area if Jim does not move, and since he is a family man, he surely has a responsibility to his family to at least maintain, if not improve their standard of living.

From the manager's point of view all these may be good arguments for moving, but they are all a reflection of some value, or some attitude to work or family, which may or may not be attractive to the other person. If they do not fit with Jim's values, the risk is that the argument may upset, offend or even make him angry. This will not help to maintain a good working relationship even short-term, let alone help with the purpose of getting him to Leicester.

The effective interviewer will, in the context of the purpose and the chosen outcome, try to consider the values, expectations and needs of the interviewee, both in his role and as a person. Normally in work we know quite a lot about the people who work for us, but we sometimes get surprises even with people we have known a long time.

What do we know about Jim?

We know that he is very competent, and we can assume that as the project manager he would be committed to the direct ordering project. We know he is worried about the health of one of his children, and at the age of 30 we can assume that the children are quite young (in real life of course you would almost certainly know). At this age it is not unusual for a man to be on the one hand quite ambitious about his work, but also to feel a very strong sense of family responsibility, especially with three children. All this is assumption at the moment, and if you really knew as little about the man as this, you would have to choose an outcome which would allow you to find out about what is important to him: ensure that he knows about the move and find out what his attitude would be and what problems would have to be overcome to enable him to move to Leicester. Even if you know the person quite well and have many more facts at your fingertips, be careful that you do not make assumptions if this is a new situation. It is too easy to jump to conclusions. Once you start to find out what his attitude is you will begin to get not only factual data, but also information about his values, needs and expectations which will help you to decide on the best strategy. Sitting back and listening will also give you time to think!

If we now look at the case from Jim's point of view we get clues as to his values, attitudes, needs and expectations:

------▶

VALUES, ATTITUDES AND NEEDS: THE SUBORDINATE

You are a project manager working for John Murdock who is the senior manager in the Management Services Department. It has been unofficially known for some time that the department is moving to another site, 160 miles away near the warehouse in Leicester. You are leading an important project, which will last at least another year, and you would expect to be asked to move with the department.

You are not very keen on moving. In fact you don't want to go! A similar job would be hard to find locally, but you are happy living where you do, and would be prepared to take other work locally as long as it paid a reasonable salary, in order to stay put.

You are 30 years old, married, with three children. The youngest of these, aged 2, was born with an abdominal condition which has already meant a number of surgical operations with the possibility of more to come. To move the child and start again at another hospital when you have built up confidence in the consultant is something you would not willingly do. For the child's sake, your wife is also very much against the move. Her family lives locally, and when the child has been ill she has gained considerable support from them.

You are well established in a local church and not only do you enjoy the friendships that you have there but you have found the church a great support.

------▶

When we look at the story from the other person's point of view we can see that many of the arguments which the manager might reasonably put forward, based on his values, are not going to be attractive to Jim. It is likely that he is committed to the project and would like to see it through, but unless something changes, it is most unlikely that he will move to Leicester on a permanent basis. Most of the other arguments will clash with his values and needs as a person, so that although he would like to move to meet his role needs (in work), he will be offended by such arguments.

It follows in this case that the most likely way for the manager to achieve his purpose is to choose an outcome which enables him to find out what is important to Jim in this situation, then to set a further outcome which is linked to his values, attitudes, needs and expectations. This means that in the first interview the senior manager would aim to ensure that Jim knows what is going to happen, and asks for his initial reaction. There would be no need to try to answer any of the problems at this stage, but by listening carefully the manager would be able to put himself in a better position for the next interview. If the interview is finished by sending Jim away to talk further with his wife, and to return with a list of the problems that would need to be overcome, this would feel caring and supportive, and would certainly not clash with his values. It would also keep the discussion open, and since he is needed for the project this is important.

At a second interview, when Jim was clearer about the problems and had discussed them with his wife, they might have changed. For example, it could become clear that he would like to see the project through to its completion but would not be able to move. The logical step might be to suggest that he commutes and stays in Leicester several nights a week, and in a year's time the whole domestic situation could be very different. The needs of the boss are met, and in a way that will not clash with the values and needs of the subordinate.

What is clear from this case is that logical argument alone is unlikely to lead to effective interviewing, and that each person will bring into the interview their own values, which needs to be recognised if the manager is to be successful.

Values, attitudes, needs and expectations will affect the interview

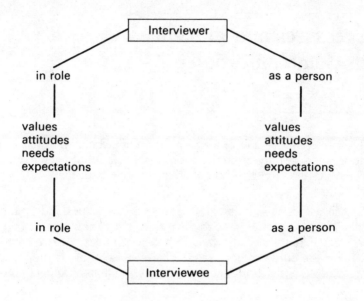

CHAPTER SIX

------------------------------------➤

Pressures and Influences in Communication

'I get the purpose and outcome clear, I understand what has to be done, and I get myself in the appropriate role – but people always behave differently! Can I do anything to help with that?'

People will behave differently because of the values and attitudes they have. As you work with them and get to know them, you can to some extent make allowance for their attitudes and use them to achieve the outcome you want. What we also know is that people are capable of behaving quite differently in different kinds of interviews.

- Why is it that when discussing a technical problem this person is so forthcoming, but in a meeting to discuss the organisation of the department they have nothing to say?
- Why is it that 'off the record' the departmental representative can seem so reasonable, but in the formal interview can be quite impossible?
- Why is it that the newly appointed supervisor who had all the right ideas at the selection interview, is heavy-handed and upsets people when it comes to handling staff?
- Why is it that the operator who has so much to say out on the shop floor can be so tongue-tied in your office?
- Why is it that even though you handled that appraisal with George in exactly the same way as the one with Martin, George was all upset while Martin thought it was very useful?

If you think about John Murdock interviewing Jim Eaton in the previous case study, it is as though John is not only having to deal with Jim and his problems, but through Jim, his wife and children as well. Not only that, but his wife's family and the church will also be influential in the outcome of the interview. We call these the

pressures and influences which affect the interview, and they have to be recognised and managed. It may be the case that these 'external' influences are more important than anything else, but if they are understood they can be very helpful in achieving the desired outcome.

There are sometimes a whole number of pressures or influences which will be significant, but it is our experience that in most cases one or two are much more significant than the others. It is these that have to be taken into account. When you know the people you work with, or those who report to you, it is often possible to 'map' out the influences that will be important in a specific interview.

If we look at boss/subordinate interviews some of the pressures or influences that might be important are:

- their own staff
- their peers
- their career
- beliefs about their own job competence
- their professional standards
- other managers for whom they are doing work
- their personal or domestic situation
- their membership of other organisations.

When we look at specific interviews we will identify others, but it will be useful to look at the effect these could have.

Their own staff

It may not be easy for a supervisor to say to their boss that they do not know how to pass some information on to their staff, or that they would not feel comfortable handling the questions that will arise. They may feel that the staff will take advantage of some change that is being brought in, but to say so would seem like a direct criticism of the boss. If the boss knows that this is the situation, it follows that the information should be given to the supervisor in a way that helps him to deal with the staff problems. If the manager does not realise that it will be a problem for the supervisor, the symptoms of the pressure will come out by the supervisor arguing with the information, or wanting to delay the implementation of the change. If this is uncharacteristic, the boss should find out if dealing with the staff on this issue will present any difficulties, and then modify the outcome from simply passing on the information to enabling the supervisor to pass it on to their staff.

Their peers

This can be internally generated ('What will my colleagues think of me if I agree and accept this idea?') or it can be overt pressure applied by the colleagues ('You cannot agree to that, the consequences for us would be ...'). If this pressure is recognised, it may suggest ways that you can present the information, or you may even have to invite questions or criticism, so that you can bring the pressure into the open. There may be no need to argue, if you achieve your purpose.

Their career

It is surprising how some people feel that it is impossible to question, let alone argue with the boss, without limiting their career opportunities. Many senior managers have talked to us about how much they are protected by their subordinates from criticism. The subordinates will filter information, and present it in the best possible way. This is often a reflection of their belief that if anything adverse is said, it will not be good for their career. The result can be that an interview is a very bland affair, or that the subordinate accepts things without question, the risk being that they may not fully understand what they are being asked to do.

Beliefs about their own job competence

Many people's jobs are central to their identities and they like to feel that they can do that job well. It is all right when you are new to a job to admit to having weaknesses and difficulties, but there comes a point when you and everyone else expect you to be competent. Then criticism, or even implied criticism, can for some people be very difficult to accept. This can be a real problem in work review and appraisal interviews, which often have built into them the expectation that the boss will criticise the person's ability to do the job. It is not surprising that these are approached by people very defensively. It is also not surprising that many companies have moved away from appraisals which are centred on personal characteristics, and adopted systems which are more focused on planning improvements for the future. Even so, it is often necessary to use the 'beliefs about job competence' by spending much more time in the appraisal reviewing the good work that has been done, and supporting the things that the person does well. If you concentrate on the problems, you run the risk of provoking an argument, or at least resentment, with people who have a strong need to believe in their own competence.

Their professional standards

At all levels people set themselves standards about what they believe is a good or acceptable piece of work. Sometimes this is laid down by the professional institutions and good practice is taught in the professional training. Standards are also built up on the factory floor and in the office. Indeed this is exactly what total quality programmes are trying to do, so that everyone plays their part in maintaining the product or service quality. In many cases the pressure that you will put on people if you ask them to do something which is against their professional standards is obvious. If you ask an accountant to do something which they consider unprofessional, it would be very difficult for them. It is less clear sometimes when you ask a computer specialist to do something which they know will mean cutting corners, or could lead to problems with another programme at a later date. The pressure you may be putting on them is only to get things done quickly, and the resistance may be expressed in terms of asking for more time. It is easy to interpret that as laziness or fussiness, when in fact you may be asking them to do an 'unprofessional' job. As trainers we are very often asked to undertake a piece of work in an afternoon, when we know it needs two or three days. Our professional standards mean that we have been known to conclude such an interview by saying that we do not want the business on those terms.

Other managers for whom they are doing work

It is not unusual for someone in an organisation involved in project work, or in a service role, to be working for several senior people. If you are requesting some work, and for you the request is perfectly reasonable, but you are getting some resistance, it may be that they do not know how to say that they are under a lot of pressure from another manager and do not know how to fend them off in order to meet your request. If you take the attitude that this is their problem to sort out and nothing to do with you, all that you do is increase the pressures. It may be the answer, but more often it leads to agreement at the time but no results. It may be necessary to help them resolve their problems with the other senior person and realistically to fit in your demands with theirs.

Their personal or domestic situation

There are many factors that could affect an interview which, on the face of it, has nothing to do with personal or domestic matters. You may decide to ask your secretary to take on some extra work which you are fairly confident she will not want to do. However, although she has said nothing to you, her personal life is much more settled than it has been for some time, and she agrees to take on the work without question. Equally, on another occasion you may ask a subordinate to stay late on a particular evening, and find that there are all sorts of arguments coming up about the project and about the overtime being worked on that evening. These arguments are from a person who is normally very co-operative, and does not mind working overtime. You cannot know that he has promised to take his mother to see a flower show, and that if the trip is cancelled she will go on about it for the next three months, and regard it as definite proof that her son has stopped loving her. The person may well feel that to say to the boss, 'I cannot do an evening's overtime on this important project because I am taking my mother to a flower show,' will sound a bit weak. However, the thought of the nagging mother may make him feel weak, and the argument will seem much more attractive. There is no way, as the manager, that you can predict this, but when there is such unusual behaviour in an interview it may be possible to listen very carefully to what is being said and pick up clues that it has to do with something personal. It is all too easy to attribute this to lack of commitment, or awkwardness, or more likely that he is in a very strange mood today.

Membership of other organisations

There are some people who are almost solely committed to work, but most people belong to other organisations or other groups. While most of the time they are able to keep them separate, there are times when those other organisations become an influence or a pressure which affects a particular interview. The obvious ones are the time demands. If you are asking someone to do some extra work on an evening which is their night for squash club, or an evening when they are expected at a meeting of the parish council, the influence may lead to a straightforward refusal or questioning the need for extra work. It may provoke a blocking of suggestions, which could lead to the person having to resolve difficulties at a later date. Sometimes this can result from a person belonging to more than one organisation within work. Most obviously this can happen with membership of a trade union. This can lead to arguments being put forward which have nothing to do with the purpose of the interview, but the person is seeing their significance for their other role in the union. It can also happen in interdepartmental meetings. Points are brought up which are not relevant to that meeting, but are to do with maintaining the department's point of view on other issues.

------→

MR JONES, THE SHOP STEWARD: PRESSURES AND INFLUENCES

You are the union shop steward in a small factory, and you have been asked by one of your members to represent him at a meeting with the production manager, Mr Edwards.

Your member, a Mr Shaw, who is an operator on the shop floor, has been dismissed for fighting with another operator, named Williams, who is also one of your members. Mr Williams has been suspended for five days without pay. There are twenty members in the section to which Mr Williams and Mr Shaw belong. You were elected shop steward about three months ago, and there are not many opportunities to represent your members except in very routine matters. You have spoken to the local official about getting more involved in union matters, and he has said you should get some more experience and then talk to him again.

Your union is the only one on site and the majority of the workforce are members. You attend disciplinary hearings only if your member requests your presence. It is written in the work rules, which are given to every new employee, that fighting is an offence for which summary dismissal is justified.

You have not had much to do with Mr Edwards, as in general the industrial relations climate has been good. When you have met him, he has usually been a reasonable man to deal with.

You are going to interview Mr Shaw before your meeting with Mr Edwards, so that you can find out exactly what happened.

------→

What are the pressures and influences that may affect Mr Jones in this interview with Mr Shaw?

Mr Jones is relatively new to his job as shop steward and one of the pressures may be that he feels uncertain about his competence to do the job. At the same time, because he wants to get more involved in union affairs, he will want to be seen to do a good job, in the eyes of the local official. Being newly elected, there would also be a pressure to be seen to be doing a good job by the members.

On balance these influences are probably working for Mr Shaw, since there is a lot that would push Mr Jones to do a good job for him, in spite of any doubts he may have about his ability to do the job.

On the other hand, there is the unequal treatment of Mr Williams, which looks like victimisation. Mr Jones would feel another pressure in fighting that one, since he could lose Mr Williams his job as well. A shop steward would often hold a value about fairness and the unequal treatment of the two would prove a pressure in itself, which might lead to an emotional rather than a rational response.

There is also the good industrial relations climate, which it would not be in anybody's interest to upset. Mr Jones has a reasonable relationship with Mr Edwards. The rules are well known, and it is standard procedure that every employee is notified that fighting is a dismissible offence.

On the face of it these influences do not help Mr Shaw's case, and they are all pressures which Mr Jones will have to carry into this interview.

In real life they would be influenced by the values, attitudes and needs that Mr Jones holds. If, for example, the pressures to do with being newly elected and proving himself in the job are the strongest, it will be difficult for him to listen to Mr Shaw with an open mind. He will tend to hear the things which give him a strong case and ignore the contrary evidence. In the end what happens in the interview may have more to do with those pressures and influences than the facts of the case.

PRESSURES AND INFLUENCES AFFECT BOTH MANAGER AND INTERVIEW

The manager, or the interviewer, is just as much subject to pressures and influences. It is important to understand what they are, and to try to understand what effect they might have on the outcome of the interview.

Some of the same influences will be there. The manager will have personal or domestic pressures, career needs, concerns about job competence, professional standards, and the other subordinates in

Typical influences on a subordinate

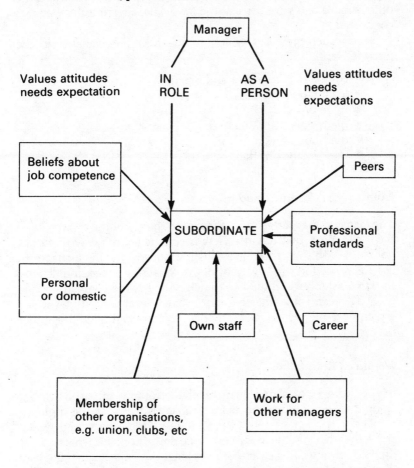

the situation. In dealing with a subordinate the manager may feel that poor performance will reflect on his own competence, career, or professional standards, and it may result in his being less understanding than he might be. We know from the work we have done on appraisal training that many managers feel that they reward the high performer, and not the average performer, but the statistics show that this is often not the case. The rewards are much more evenly spread. This is because the pressure in the appraisal interview will come from having to justify a higher reward to one person than to another. In what feels like a subjective area, this influences the manager to treat the subordinates in the same way. It is as if the other subordinates are there at the interview, affecting the way it is conducted.

Some other pressures which could affect the manager in the interview are:

- company procedures and practices
- legal requirements
- trade unions
- the organisation's culture
- their boss
- the demands of their own job.

Company procedures and practices

The manager may agree or disagree with them, but the awareness of them will mean that the interview is conducted in a way that does not clash with the procedures. It is not unusual for the manager to use the procedures as a way of de-personalising a decision: 'Under the circumstances I would like to help you, but the company policy is …' This can sometimes be very useful, but at other times it is a screen to hide behind and can be very frustrating to the other person.

Legal requirements

In the business of staff management there has been an increasing amount of legislation, and many managers feel that the 'right to manage' has been eroded. Of course there are others who would argue that there is a need for employee protection, but whatever the rights or wrongs, it is clear that people will be influenced in the way they conduct their interviews by the presence of the legislation. The fear of finding oneself justifying a decision in an industrial tribunal can be a pressure, which leads to some situations not being confronted. It is our experience that some organisations are more sensitive about the legislation, while others are prepared to take greater risks.

Trade unions

These can have a similar effect on staff management interviews. Even on our courses where we use some case studies with an industrial relations content, it is possible to see that there are some managers who are afraid of trade unions. The decisions they take are influenced by that fear. This is usually the case when a manager has little experience of working with the unions, or comes from a background with poor industrial relations. However, sometimes the influence can be very positive and helpful to achieving the desired outcome. In a disciplinary interview, if a manager knows that the union will back them if there is a fair case, then this can provide some strength to the manager conducting such an interview.

The organisation's culture

By this we simply mean the way things are done in one organisation differently to another. We know that the idea of organisation culture is much more complex than that, but for this purpose that definition will suffice. It is usually only when you go to another organisation that you become aware of the culture in your own. It is like going to France and realising that not everyone queues. Even within a large organisation there may be different cultures in different establishments. Our favourite example is that in one part of a large company when people were off sick or away for any other reason more than a certain number of times, they were sacked. People from the same organisation, but a different establishment, could not believe it and would argue fiercely that this could not be done. However, the amazement was mutual, because the sacking managers found it difficult to comprehend this reaction, as they did sack people and it was seen as normal practice.

There are certainly some cultures where to have to discipline anyone is seen as a failure, because it should have been possible to deal with the problem in some other way. In some informal cultures there is pressure to deal with most things as if they were a 'chat', which is very unhelpful for achieving some outcomes, such as disciplinary. In other cultures it is almost bad form to say anything directly, and mistakes are alluded to rather than discussed.

For example, a report of a crisis during the night in a hospital and the subsequent interview between the consultant and the administrator concerned reads:

> The meeting was quite brief, and for the administrator relatively undistressing – perhaps reflecting the health service's tradition of civilised administration. It was agreed between the two men that 'serious teething troubles' still existed, and that much more time would be spent sorting out the problem.

These are not the kind of words that would be used in some factories we know, but it does not follow that the interviews would be any more or less effective, simply that the problems would be dealt with in different ways. When people work in new places they have to learn the appropriate way to behave in the new culture, and this often means getting it wrong, and then being told. We may find it difficult to articulate what is right and what is wrong in the culture, but it is very clear when it is wrong.

Their boss

The boss can be a very important influence in the way interviews are conducted. Managers are often asked by their own boss to do something with which they do not wholly agree, or in some cases, with which they disagree. The manager knows that the boss will follow up the instruction, and may even ask in detail what happened at the interview. This can be a positive pressure, meaning that the manager feels the strength of the boss behind him. Knowing that he has backing and authority enables him to carry through the toughest interview.

However, on other occasions what their boss is asking them to do will upset the relationships they have with their subordinates and put the manager in a stressful position. This often happens when their boss is newly appointed and asks for things to be done in different ways. The new boss may also have strong views on a particular subject, which then influences interviews. For example, as part of an assignment, we were looking at the appraisal forms for a division of a particular company. We noticed that almost everyone needed to improve their communication skills. We could not believe this to be true, and further investigation made it clear that the divisional manager had a 'bee in his bonnet' about communications. The result was an influence, which he had certainly not intended, on nearly all the appraisals of his people.

The demands of the manager's job

Managers are usually busy with a wide range of tasks, many of which are short-term or priority tasks, which will influence their interviews. Sometimes the deadline will mean that the manager cannot afford the time and may seem impatient. For example, if there is an important customer waiting for an answer, it may push the manager into being executive and making a decision, rather than working through the problem with the subordinate.

These are some examples of the pressures that a manager may carry into an interview, and they can affect the way it is conducted. It is important that the interviewer is aware of the pressures, so that they can be identified and managed, especially when they will be unhelpful to the achievement of the desired outcome.

The manager in this position may realise that the interview is with the wrong person. It would be more appropriate to have the interview with the person who is creating the pressure, and sort out some of the problems before giving them to a subordinate. Much of a manager's job is shielding subordinates from unhelpful influences that come from their boss, other departments and outside bodies, so that they can get on with their job. The good manager often thinks about those pressures and considers if they are appropriate to pass on, or if it is the manager's job to absorb them. The criteria should always be to test them in relation to purpose and outcome. We have noticed a tendency, which goes along with vague ideas about participation, to discuss unnecessary topics with subordinates. The result is that they carry the pressures as well, and this can be very debilitating and confusing.

▶

MR BLAKE – PRESSURES ON THE BOSS

You are Mr Blake, a development manager. Your department has a variety of projects concerning the development of processes rather than products. You are frequently away from the laboratory and therefore require your development engineers to be able to work on their own and to take the initiative to overcome problems as they occur.

Six months ago a development engineer, Mr Gilbert, was transferred to your department. Mr Gilbert had previously worked in another development area and while he had not worked on process development, both you and his former manager felt that his product development experience was very relevant to your department's activities. Mr Gilbert's former manager also spoke highly of his work. He was said to be conscientious and not afraid of taking the initiative, and apparently he got on well with his colleagues.

You, therefore, had high expectations of Mr Gilbert, which has perhaps heightened your sense of disappointment over the last six months. Since his arrival he has shown few of the qualities he was reputed to have. You have found it difficult to get him to work, and the little that he has done has come from pushing him. He has shown a marked reluctance to use his initiative, and furthermore seems to be finding it hard to work with his new colleagues. He is in fact becoming a loner. You, of course, did not expect him to fit in immediately, but feel that by now some signs of improvement should be seen. You have discussed his performance with his previous boss and the personnel officer and have found no clue to this complete change. You have therefore decided to see Mr Gilbert.

It is important that Mr Gilbert is made aware of the high standard of competence, initiative and general professionalism that you expect from your staff. A poor performance from any of your staff reflects adversely on the whole department and, of course, on you as the manager. You are very keen that your department is seen as competent and professional.

⟶

The purpose of the interview is to improve Mr Gilbert's performance, and as usual there are a number of outcomes to choose from. One could be to find out from Mr Gilbert the reasons why his performance does not seem to be up to the expected standard. Another would be to see if he perceives a problem, and if so what are the causes. Yet another would be to ensure that he knows what is expected of him, and then to agree plans to improve the situation.

One pressure on the manager is the expected professional standards. Another is the way that the department will be seen by other managers. Another could be his own career needs, since he feels that a poor performance reflects on him as the manager. Another could be the general morale of the department if it is carrying someone who does not seem to be pulling their weight, and is behaving as a loner. A further pressure might be that the manager was responsible for selecting the man, and if he is the wrong choice that will not look good. He might also feel some guilt that he is away from the laboratory so frequently, and may not have been able to give Mr Gilbert as much support as he needed.

Let us assume that Mr Blake has decided to try to find out how Mr Gilbert sees the situation, and to agree some plans to improve his performance. If he is to achieve this outcome, he will need to put on one side the pressures which will make him want to say that Mr Gilbert's work is not good enough, that he is letting down the reputation of the department, and indeed Mr Blake's personal reputation. He may need to contain his disappointment, and be careful not to blame Mr Gilbert as a poor choice. Mr Blake will need to clear his mind of all these pressures, and make sure that Mr Gilbert believes that he, as a manager, is genuinely interested in the difficulties the new employee may have had in settling into the department, and that he is really willing to help him improve. If it is possible to create this atmosphere in the interview, there is a chance that Mr Gilbert will tell his manager what problems he has, but if there is a hint of blame, he will almost certainly start to defend his actions. Once that happens there will probably be an argument, and then there will be no choice but to be executive and tell him that he has to improve.

There will be a natural tendency to slip into this executive role, given the pressures that Mr Blake has to deal with, and the outcome will almost certainly not be the selected one. What happens with the influence of these pressures is that the outcome slips from the desired one to another. Good interviewing is about managing that change, not letting it drift.

In this chapter we have identified a number of the pressures and influences that can affect interviews. They are not presented as a definitive list, but rather as examples to illustrate and reinforce the ideas.

Managerial interviews do not take place in isolation. In the main they occur within a relationship, which has a history and a future, at a time when both parties have other concerns. Inevitably these pressures and influences cannot be forgotten and may be brought into the interview. They can be helpful and supportive to achieving the outcome or they can provide blocks and hindrances to success. However, identification of the key influences is the first step towards using and managing them successfully in interviews.

Chapter Seven

Communication Skills

Using your skills more effectively

We have discussed the various components that have to be managed to make interviews effective, but in the end these are put into practice with skills. Some approaches to interviewing seem to suggest that you need special skills in order to interview. Our approach helps people in interviews to use the same skills which they use in any other social setting. Effective interviewing means recognising when to use the appropriate skills, and which skills are appropriate for the task, or the outcome which you hope to achieve.

When we were first designing this form of training, we were also involved in research on effective interviewing. For research purposes we identified some work which had been undertaken by the Department of Manpower and Immigration, in Saskatchewan, Canada. They had identified the micro-skills, the little pieces of skill which people use in social interaction. We abstracted from this list those that are used in interviews. We then translated them into questions or phrases which would enable people to review their own skills in a training situation. We have now tested this approach in many courses over a period of fifteen years, in many different companies, working with managers, specialists, consultants, salesmen and supervisors. We have also used the approach with careers officers, teachers, social workers, educational psychologists, nurses and doctors. This extensive experience has led us to believe that these skills are generic. Although we have recategorised the skills for specific types of interviews, and found that some have special importance in others, we have continued to find them valuable for people wishing to improve their interviewing.

There are three basic groups of skill:

- the skills of eliciting information
- the skills of presenting information
- the skills of managing the emotional content.

The active skills of eliciting and presenting information are subdivided to include the skills used to check and ensure that understanding and meaning has been communicated. We call these feedback skills.

All interviews will involve feelings or emotions on the part of both people. The skilled interviewer will manage the climate of the interview, recognise the feelings that are affecting the situation, and work to ensure that they do not prevent the achievement of the desired outcome.

Any interview will be a mix of eliciting skills, presenting skills, and skills of managing the emotional content. The balance will change depending on the interview. If the outcome is clear, the extent to which it can be planned is known, and the roles and pressures understood, it will often be possible to predict the balance of the skills.

If, for example you are a systems analyst trying to understand the detail of a work flow, you would expect there to be a small amount of presenting, perhaps to explain what is needed, and why the information is required, but the bulk of the interview would require the analyst to use their eliciting skills. Assuming that the person being interviewed was happy to give the information, and assuming that the analyst was confident about the task, there would probably be very little emotional content to manage.

Balance of skills in a fact-finding interview

If you were conducting an interview, in the middle of a redundancy programme, informing someone that they would not be losing their job, but that their work in future would be very different, you would expect the balance to be much more weighted towards the presenting skills and managing the emotional content.

Balance of skills in a redundancy interview

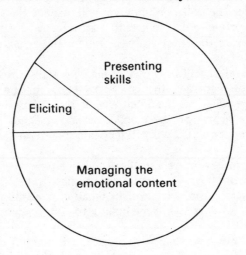

It is not always possible to predict the skill balance, but the more the interview is prescribed, the more it is possible to predict what skills will be needed. If the facts are known, if the control is with the interviewer, and it is clear what type of relationship is needed, then the balance will usually be predictable. When there is a procedure, or clear structure for the interview, it will often be clear what skills you need. In a formal disciplinary interview, you may need to control your feelings of discomfort, you may need to shut out the emotions which might be brought in by the other person, but it is clear that the demand is for presenting skills. The only questions needed will be to check that the person understands. In fact, if the manager allows any more questions, the other person will probably change the purpose of the interview.

In the less prescribed interviews the use of skills can be more complex. In a personal counselling interview the majority of skills used will be eliciting, with feedback skills to check understanding. There may be some parts where it is necessary to present information, and check that it is understood, and others where the emotional content must be managed appropriately or the person may not feel able to talk at all. It is not only the interviewee who needs the emotional content to be managed, but the interviewer as well, since their feelings will affect their ability to use their other skills effectively.

Balance of skills in a formal disciplinary interview

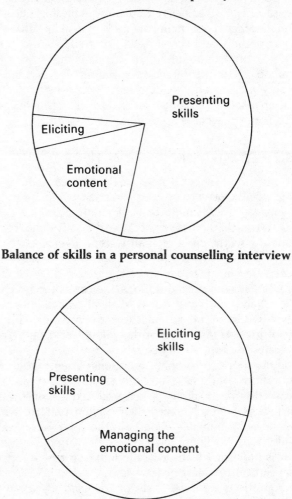

Balance of skills in a personal counselling interview

This planning is important because under the pressure of the meeting, it is not unusual for people to know that the interview is primarily about finding the facts, but to go through it hardly asking a question. Most people know what it is like to go to a selection interview and to come out feeling that the interviewer does not know very much about them. In fact, if you think back, they probably did most of the talking. If you ask them the reason, they will usually rationalise it in terms of having to give the candidate information about the organisation. Of course this is true, but there are often better ways of doing it, and it should certainly not be at the expense of the other desired outcome – finding out about the candidate. Another common imbalance is in deciding that the interview is fact-finding, and therefore eliciting skills are required, but not doing enough presenting to explain the reason for the questions. So often the interviewer makes the assumption that because they are clear why a question is being asked, it will be clear to the other person. Without that understanding, it may be very difficult to know at what level of detail to answer it.

THE SKILLS OF ELICITING INFORMATION

Skills are not good or bad things in themselves; they are simply tools which can be used to achieve something in an interview. The form of question used is important. Open questions are often very useful for starting a discussion, because they give the interviewee choices about how the question is answered. An example of an open question would be, 'How do you see your career developing?' This can be answered in great detail or at a general level. If the interviewer continues with open questions, the content may remain at a general level and never get down to detail. Sometimes the interviewee will find them difficult questions to answer, simply because they do not give an indication of the amount of detail required, or what aspect of the topic is to be discussed.

Specific questions, or probing questions, often follow the open starter questions, and these are often formed out of the other person's words. For example, 'When you said a moment ago that some customers were changing their buying pattern, which customers were you thinking about?' If the interviewer only asks specific questions, it will not feel like a conversation, but more like a grilling. It is important to bear this in mind, so that an appropriate emotional climate is maintained.

Closed questions are those that only demand a yes or no for an answer, and they are particularly useful for checking assumptions. For example, 'When you said that you have an evening commitment, does that mean that you are unable to work any overtime?' Closed questions are a favourite tool of lawyers in court because they give them control over the witness' answer. A long question, which specifies all the information and can only be answered yes or no can be very useful. 'So would you say that the only way that this advertising will be successful is to let the agency handle it, to ensure that they work within the budget, and for us to monitor it on a monthly basis?' If this form of question is over-used, it can be just as frustrating for the subordinate or colleague as it is for the witness, who feels unable to say what he really wants to.

Another form of question which we observe very frequently is the multiple question. This is two, three or sometimes four questions all asked one after the other without waiting for a reply. This is particularly common if the interviewer is feeling uncertain about their task, and uncertain about how the interviewee is going to respond. It also occurs if the interviewer has a low tolerance to silence. There only needs to be a suggestion of hesitation, and the questions come tumbling out. It is a great pity, since all of the questions are often important, and some of them will go unanswered. Frequently the first question was a very relevant one, requiring some thought before giving an answer, and it was this that produced the hesitation. Multiple questioning is a habit that some people get into, and what it does is to 'waste' the good skills which are lost with the unanswered questions.

If the interview is going well, or the person is talking about something easily, it is often not necessary to ask further questions, but simply to encourage them to keep talking with well positioned 'supporting statements'. You will find that you have your own which you use quite naturally, and they are a mix of non-verbal nods and smiles, grunts, ums and ahs, and phrases such as 'that's interesting' or 'I see'. The important thing is not so much what is said but that it expresses interest and is timed so that it supports what is being said rather than cutting the person off.

Some feedback skills are to do with recognising what is happening in the interview. It is important to be watching for the effect of the questions that are used. It may be that they were not understood, either because the words were unfamiliar, or they were interpreted in terms of the other person's frame of reference. The recognition will come from listening to the answer, and trying to understand how they interpreted the question. The question may also be answered at an unexpected level of detail, or it may become clear that their approach to the subject is different from yours. Sometimes the person will say that they do not know how to answer the question in that form, because they have not thought of it like that before. More often there will be an attempt to answer the question, and the interviewer must interpret the answer.

Recognising when a person finds it difficult to express or give information is an important skill. It seems that this hesitation, or struggling to express an idea, often means that the person is having to think more deeply. This may be indicative that the interview has moved to a more significant subject, or that the discussion is closer to the centre of the problem, rather than the previous topics which were discussed without any great thought. Of course it may also be indicative that the questions were obtuse or difficult for the interviewee, but in either case it is significant feedback.

A similar point is the need to recognise when someone is unable or unwilling to give further information. We have argued for analysis and preparation of interviews, but the skilled interviewer also needs to be sensitive to the fact that their well-thought-out questions may be something that the person is unwilling to answer. To continue with them will certainly make the interviewee feel uneasy, even resentful, or if they are unable to answer, foolish. This, of course, can influence the rest of the interview.

The active skills to encourage feedback are summarising the points made by the other person, asking them which points were fact and which opinion, and checking your understanding by expressing the idea in your own words. These skills are important if you want to avoid the risk of making inaccurate assumptions.

Summarising is useful not only to check that you have got the main points, but also to assure the other person that you have been listening. It often means that you will get more information, because the interviewee will add to or correct a matter of emphasis in your summary. It is also an important way of controlling the pace of the interview. In many fact-finding interviews you will find that you are given a great deal of information, and you need to slow the process down so that you can assimilate and retain the information. You can give some control to the interview by summarising as you go along, not just at the end. A summary can be followed by a question that directs the interviewee to the next area that you would like to know about, thus controlling the topics discussed.

Checking that your perceptions are right by expressing the idea in your own words is another way in which the two-way communication process is encouraged. Again it helps the person know that you have been listening, but it will also give you the confidence that the two of you are talking about the same thing, even if you use different words.

These feedback skills are vital for successful counselling and consulting interviews. They are also important as a means of control in interviews where the other person is upset or angry, or needs someone to talk through a problem. These skills not only reassure the interviewer that they have understood, they assure the interviewee that they have been heard. They may also encourage further thought. The feedback says 'this is the message you have given me', and that may promote the thought that it is not quite like that, allowing the interviewee to try to express it in another way. This is often the process by which someone will solve something for himself, and is therefore an important skill for a manager.

CHECKLIST OF SKILLS FOR ELICITING INFORMATION

Managing the interview towards the desired outcome by

- obtaining information by the use of questions

    Open questions:
    How is the new member of the salesforce fitting in?
    What do you think we should do to launch the new product?

    Specific questions:
    What percentage of target did you achieve last month?
    Who is responsible for checking the returns?

    Closed questions:
    Do you want to change the advertising?
    Did the samples arrive on time?

- by asking closed questions to check your own and the other person's assumptions
- encouraging communication by using supporting statements such as 'That's interesting, I see, tell me more, uh huh ...'
- demonstrating to the other person that you were listening, for example by using their words to form questions
- identifying the main points made by the other person, and how they differ from yours
- distinguishing fact from opinion in the other person's statements

Eliciting information – feedback skills

What effect did the questions have on the interview and the achievement of the purpose?

- Were the questions understood?

- Were they answered at the appropriate level of detail?
- Was the approach to the subject different?

Recognise events in the interview, where the other person found it difficult to express or give information

Recognise when the person is unable or unwilling to give information

Check understanding by summarising the main points made by the other person

Check with the other person what was fact and what was opinion

Check your perception by expressing the ideas in your own words.

THE SKILLS OF PRESENTING INFORMATION

Since it is of major importance that the purpose of the interview is clear, a key skill is stating that purpose. Of course, there are occasions when it would not be advantageous to explain the purpose of an interview, but generally the purpose will need to be explained, and it will need to be agreed. In fact, if this is not done, both people may, with the best will in the world, be working against each other.

Another skill is directing the conversation towards the desired outcome, which implies that the interviewer is very clear what that outcome will be. The acid test for anything that has to be presented is that it must contribute directly to that outcome. It is too easy to bring in other points, which may be relevant, but which over-complicate the interview, hindering the achievement of the out-come.

There are usually choices about the sequence in which items are presented, and how they are organised. We will discuss the sequences for particular interviews later, but the general skill is to present items in the sequence which will take the listener from where they are in their knowledge at present, to where you want them to be. It is important to think about the sequence from the listener's point of view rather than the interviewer's.

As with the eliciting skills, where it is useful to build questions out of what has been said, it is also useful to take the ideas which have already been presented, and build the next point on to that. This will help to consolidate the first point, and build a connection in the other person's mind to the subsequent one. It can be enhanced by using summarising skills to consolidate the information and give the listener time to think before moving on to the next topic.

If you are presenting something which is slanted in a particular way because of certain assumptions you are making, or values which you hold, then it may help to clarify why you give emphasis to these points and not others, by making it clear that it is your point of view.

The feedback skills are important to check the effectiveness of what you have presented. There is not much point in telling your subordinate to do something, unless you are sure that it has been heard, and understood in the way that you intended. That is the purpose of these skills. It is surprising how many managers work on the assumption that because they said something, it must have been understood. The clues for understanding come from the questions or points that are made in response to the presented information, but the good interviewer will be active in checking this, rather than relying on the other person saying when it is not clear.

They will use questions which ask the other person to make it clear if they accept what has been said, and they will also ask the person for evidence that it has been understood. At the lowest level this will sometimes mean asking the interviewee to recap what has been said, or to summarise the points that have been made, or it could mean asking the other person to describe what action they think would be appropriate, which will indicate what they have understood.

Another skill is to recognise the words or themes which have had particular impact. Sometimes these are topics or facts which you have not seen as particularly important, but they are picked up immediately and are obviously important to the interviewee. At other times you will think that something is going to be important, but it is something else which they have been worrying about. The importance of recognising these things is that they will bias the way that the information is heard, and may mean that the message you are trying to get over will be distorted. Of course, sometimes you will know that a theme will have a particular impact, and you can use it to get the message over, but you still need to take care to ensure that you are right.

Some people are 'economical with words' and only say things once, but if you listen to most conversations you will notice that people say something and then paraphrase it to check if it is understood. It is often the cue for the other person to say that they have understood, or make a comment on what has been said, which then allows the first person to continue. This is a skill which serves the same purpose in interviews.

This checking enables the interviewer to recognise when it is appropriate to continue, by presenting more information. At other times clues are available to show that either the interviewee has understood the point, and further discussion is not needed, or that enough has been said and the desired outcome has been reached, so that the interview can be finished.

In our experience some people are very comfortable using their presenting skills, and this means that the interviews which are concerned with passing on information, instructing people on what to do, disciplinary interviews, terminating someone's employment, or announcing a redundancy, may come easily to them. When there is a need to use the feedback skills, these same people may not find the interview so easy, but they are vital to ensure that acceptance or understanding has been achieved.

CHECKLIST OF SKILLS FOR PRESENTING INFORMATION

Explain the purpose of the interview.

Direct the conversation towards the desired outcome by

- presenting information in a sequenced and organised way,
- building on ideas previously introduced,
- introducing one idea at a time,
- clarifying fact from opinion,
- stating your personal point of view,
- building appropriate summaries into the interview.

Presenting information – feedback

Check the effectiveness of the presentation and appropriateness to the purpose of the interview by

- identifying the extent to which words and ideas are accepted,
- identifying the extent to which words and ideas are understood,
- identifying words or themes which have particular impact.

Paraphrase and watch to see if understanding is clarified.

Manage the interview towards the desired outcome by

- recognising when to continue or build on ideas which have already been introduced,
- recognising when further discussion is not needed, so that the interview can be continued or finished.

THE SKILLS OF MANAGING THE EMOTIONAL CONTENT

All interviews will have an emotional content that must be managed. We tend to use the word emotional to mean the high emotional states of anger, frustration or crying, but many other feelings will be experienced in an interview. The interviewer can feel uncomfortable when dealing with issues which are at the edge of their technical competence. The interviewee may feel tense when being asked about work which has not been completed. Most of us will have experienced the nervousness of attending a selection interview, or the sense of achievement when getting over a complicated point to someone.

Also, you will probably have witnessed someone, who knows the subject very well, 'drying up' in the middle of a presentation. The opposite is equally true, that people who are nervous or feel under stress may say things they do not mean or even intended not to say. We came across an experienced personnel manager, who started a redundancy interview with the question, 'How do you see your future with the company?' This is an extreme example of how feelings can influence what is said. What is clear is that the feelings of both people will affect the way they use their skills and, therefore, the outcome of the interview.

It is helpful for the interviewer to understand where those feelings come from. In the previous chapters we looked at the pressures and influences, and the values, attitudes and needs that each person has, which they bring into the interview. This is one source of the emotions that have to be managed.

Some feelings will be generated by the role that the person has within the organisation, or within the interview. We have already discussed how a subordinate will define that role in relation to the boss, and how this may mean, for example, that personal matters are not discussed with the boss. Other people may hold the belief that the boss should manage, and in that case ideas about participation would be very difficult. A work review could be very uncomfortable for that person. If we take another example, it is often said to people when they want promotion that they should move to another establishment or company, because here they will always be remembered as the junior.

On other occasions the role that someone has may give them the authority to do their job. It is not unusual for a security officer, who could be quite low in the hierarchy, to interview a senior executive about where he has parked his car, or some other misdemeanour which has been committed. The role of doctor will enable a person to ask personal questions, which they might feel very uncomfortable asking in a social setting. Some people carry their managerial authority into the executive role, and conduct interviews that demand this role very effectively, but the same person may be very uncomfortable in the role of counsellor, where control has to be shared. The result of the discomfort is usually that the skills are not used as effectively.

The interviewer and the interviewee are people with their own values, needs, attitudes and expectations. This means that they will feel certain issues are important or even have prejudices which generate feelings about certain types of interview. Some men expect women to behave in an emotional way in interviews. Some men just do not like interviewing women, especially in the 'tough' interviews. Some people do not feel comfortable telling other people what to do, and would much rather ask them. Some people have a need to be liked, and that makes them feel uncomfortable in certain interviews. Others have a strong belief in treating people fairly, and this can cloud their judgements. There are many factors which make us the people we are, some of which give us feelings which are helpful, some of which are not so helpful in achieving the purpose of the interview.

Another set of feelings are created by what happens in the interview itself. The atmosphere of formality or informality may make people feel comfortable or uneasy. Some subjects are much easier to discuss in an informal friendly atmosphere, but establishing that climate is not functional for all interviews, and it does not relax all interviewees. It may be that a chance remark has particular impact and upsets the interviewee; it may be that the interviewee feels threatened by a criticism and so criticises the boss. Instead of ignoring it, the boss feels threatened, starts to justify his action, and an argument starts. The purpose of the interview is lost, because the emotional climate is not managed.

Sometimes people will use emotional appeals to each other to avoid the outcome of the interview. The subordinate may say,

'Come on, John, you're surely not going to say that to me – we've worked together for all these years.' The boss may say to the subordinate, 'Well be reasonable, George, you have to see it from my point of view.' A statement like 'everyone knows that ...' makes it very difficult for someone to question it, and 'every fool knows ...' is even more difficult. All these emotional appeals will be used in interviews. They should be recognised for what they are, symptoms of discomfort. If they are responded to at an emotional level, an argument can follow, and the purpose of the interview will not be achieved. It is also quite likely that the feelings which both people take into subsequent interviews will not be helpful to their outcomes.

As these examples show, an overt attempt to influence emotions rarely has the desired effect. For instance, if someone is angry, telling them not to be angry, tends to increase, not decrease, the anger. The skills needed for managing the emotional content are skills of recognition. These enable the active skills of eliciting and presenting to be used appropriately to manage the emotions, so that the outcomes can be achieved. How this is done in specific types of interviews is more fully developed in Part 2.

CHECKLIST OF SKILLS FOR MANAGING THE
EMOTIONAL CONTENT

Managing the feelings brought into, or created in the interview, appropriately for the achievement of the desired outcome involves:

- recognising how my role influences the relationship I am trying to build
- recognising how my prejudices, attitudes and values affect the relationship and how they are managed during the interview
- recognising how the interviewee's role affects their behaviour
- identifying clues which tell me about them as a person and their attitudes.

Assessing the feelings created in the interview:

Is the climate appropriate for the purpose, and the relationship I am trying to establish?

Does it change? Why? Are the changes helping or hindering the achievement of the desired outcome?

Recognise areas where the interviewee was reticent or talked freely.

Recognise when I became uncomfortable. Why?

Recognise emotional appeals. Why were they used?

Use the interviewee's words to show that I am listening. This can help to maintain or change the appropriate emotional climate.

Summary of the Interviewing Model

Effective interviewing requires that the type of relationship and the roles, the influences and pressures on both people, the extent to which it can be planned, and the balance of skills, are managed appropriately. This means that they are managed so that the desired outcome for the specific interview is achieved, in the context of the overall purpose.

An integrated model of effective interviewing

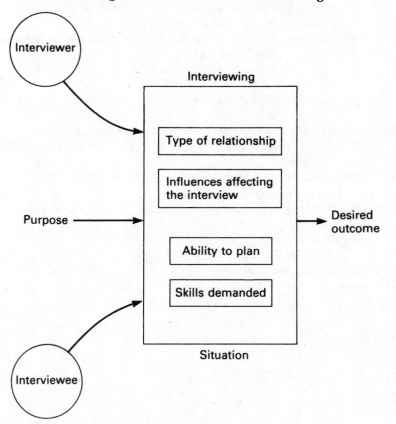

In Part 2 of the book we shall apply this model to different interviews, so that you will be able to use it practically, but if you have read this chapter you will probably be able to use the checklist below to improve your interviews. It uses this model, but translates it into questions which will help you to plan interviews of all types, and to consider the interrelationship between the components which we have discussed in this chapter.

MANAGING DIFFERENT INTERVIEWS EFFECTIVELY

- What is the purpose of the interview?
- Are there significant events which have led to the necessity to hold the interview?
- What is the desired outcome for me?
  What do I imagine it is for the other person?
- Can I/should I prepare for the interview?
  Are there facts I should be familiar with?
  Is it important that the control stays with me?
- What kind of relationship should I build during the interview? Do I have a choice?
- Given the purpose, and the desired outcome, what is likely to be the need for:
  presenting skills
  eliciting skills
  attention to and management of the emotional climate?
- What demands and pressures will be on me during the interview?
  In what way will they affect me?
  Will they affect the outcome?
- What demands and pressures do I think will be on the other person?
  How will they influence them?
  Is it important that I do something during the interview to take account of these?

PART TWO

BRINGING ABOUT CHANGE
THROUGH OTHER PEOPLE

CHAPTER EIGHT

Managing Change

One of the questions we are most frequently asked on our Interviewing and Appraisal Courses is 'How do I get so-and-so to change?' This normally means either getting them to stop doing something, accepting new ideas and responsibilities or changing the way they do an existing task.

In the last few years so much emphasis has been placed on the management of change with increasing competition, accelerating technological change and the information revolution. This has produced a whole series of books, both academic and based on personal experiences, on how to manage change in organisations, but there are few books on individual change. We find this somewhat surprising, not because the books on organisation change are valueless – on the contrary many are excellent – but because it is a partial view. In fact, the majority of managers are not engaged in bringing about vast changes in organisations, but in overcoming a subordinate's resistance to a new idea, improving his department's efficiency, introducing a new system or technology, increasing flexibility or developing his staff. It is true many of these may take place within the context of a larger organisation change, but the focus is departmental or individual.

Change and the manager's role

The manager's role has changed with the changing organisational environment and with the need to be more market-aware. No longer is the bureaucratic virtue of adherence to rules valued, as the needs for responsiveness and flexibility are prized. The emphasis is not on compliance with procedures, but on development and more freedom to act within clearly stated parameters. In this sense almost all managers' interviews are to do with managing changes.

An appraisal interview, for example, may require a rating of last year's performance for salary purposes, and it is important that the appraisee leaves the interview, not only with a balanced view of his or her performance, but also of how that relates to his/her job in the coming period. To concentrate on a development need such as project planning, when the emphasis for the job in the future is on overcoming implementation problems, will not set the right priorities for the subordinate. This would be the case even if the implementation problems were due to poor planning. You would need the subordinate to understand this, but would not spend excessive time developing plans to overcome the problems. Instead you would be more pragmatic in developing solutions to aid the implementation, recognising the need for better planning on the next project.

Another example would be work review – say a manager and his supervisor reviewing last month's production figures against plan. Typically the differences between planned and actual performance would be studied. Why? One of the reasons would be to identify what had happened and the reasons for this, not so that blame could be apportioned, but to learn how to tackle similar problems in the future. In this way by the positive reinforcement of what has worked and by identifying problems and possible solutions, the manager develops and changes his department and supervisor. If the subordinate feels you are concentrating on the problems and it feels like apportioning blame, then he will tend to take few risks and become resistant to change as he will think the risks are his alone.

➤ A CASE OF WORK REVIEW

You are the regional sales manager for a company which produces and sells cakes and biscuits. The cake and biscuit market is changing. More and more of the market is being concentrated in the major supermarket chains and less being sold in local stores. This is a highly competitive sector of the business. Centralised buying cuts your margin, your competitors are very active as the business is so large, some of the supermarket chains will only buy the brand leaders and an increasing share of the market is being taken by supermarket own brands, which your company, for policy reasons, will not supply. To safeguard and increase the turnover, the company has recently introduced two new product ranges, a range of luxury biscuits, which is felt to be an underdeveloped sector of the market, and a range of large individually packed biscuits, which it is hoped will compete with chocolate bars in the snack/confectionery markets.

You are about to have a monthly sales meeting with one of your salesmen, Michael Stavros. You transferred Michael to his current area about a year ago, on the retirement of another salesman. The area was not performing as well as it should and you felt Michael, a good competent salesman, would increase sales, which in fact he has, averaging now 20 per cent more sales than a year ago.

The sales figures you are about to review are for June. They are presented on page 86.

Looking at the figures you make the following judgements:

1. The cake market continues to be depressed for a series of reasons that you have already discussed with Michael over the last few months. Given this his performance last month looks good, in fact the best of your salesmen.
2. Biscuits. What is happening to 'creams'? Coconut chip still is underperforming. The new luxury range is doing well. Individual biscuits: he achieved his budget, but his sales were low relative to your other salesmen. The trend to new cheese biscuits seems to be continuing.
3. Accounts closing is outnumbering new accounts.
4. Overall a good month and showing the continuing build up of business in the area, although this now appears to be slowing down.

Let's now think about the meeting with Michael. What is its purpose? To review last month's sales figures. Compare this meeting with the example of an exit interview on page 20. Again it is liable to be a routine or regular meeting, the sales manager and Michael meet every month, they may even follow the same way of looking at the figures. It is in circumstances like these, when regular meetings become routine, that the purpose can often be merely implied or, even worse, lost altogether.

We would maintain that 'to review last month's sales figures' is not a purpose. It is something you may well do in an interview, but why? It is the answer to this question that gives you an indication of the purpose. As we mentioned earlier, the real reason for reviewing work is to learn from the past, in order to improve performance in the future. Given then that the sales manager's purpose is for Michael to improve the sales performance in his area, what specific outcomes does he want from reviewing June's sales figures?

These will fall into two areas. Firstly, ideas, information and possible actions the manager may want or need to take. For instance, what is the salesman's view of introducing new cheese

Sales Figures for June

PRODUCT		TARGET VOLUME FOR MONTH	SALES	% TARGET	YEAR TO DATE SALES	% BUDGET
CAKES	Fruit	190	200	105	1458	101
	Ginger	350	330	94	2150	94
	Cherry	350	330	94	2160	90
	Coconut	180	170	94	1200	90
	Pies	400	380	95	2300	92
	Individual	310	300	97	2100	93
BISCUITS	Chocolate Covered	720	720	100	4500	98
	Digestive	1050	1100	105	6400	102
	Cream	250	200	80	1310	85
	Chocolate Chip	500	520	104	3120	100
	Coconut Chip	280	270	96	1600	94
	Nut Chip	390	400	102	2420	98
	Luxury	80	85	106	240*	105
	Individual	38	38	100	105*	101
CHEESE BISCUITS	Crackers	1100	1080	99	6540	98
	Crispbreads	780	880	112	5300	105

Account changes during month
New Accounts 4
Accounts Closed 6

* Last 3 months

biscuits to take advantage of a possible switch in consumer taste?
Secondly what does the manager want Michael to concentrate on in
the following month?

In this case, while the overall performance is good, there is a
slight concern over the new individual biscuit, particularly in relation to new accounts. The product after all was introduced to
compete in the confectionery/snack market, enabling your products
to get access to outlets, which had traditionally not stocked biscuits.
The manager, therefore, would need an outcome specific to the
relationship between the new product and new accounts. Whether
this is left as simply that Michael understands the importance of
new accounts, or a target for new accounts is set, or an agreed plan
for how the new accounts will be established, will depend upon
their relationship and the manager's judgement of Michael's ability
to perform. The important point is that without the specific outcome, the danger is that Michael will rely on his proven ability to
increase sales with present customers, rather than investing his time
and energy on developing new accounts.

$$\longrightarrow$$

RESISTANCE TO CHANGE

If the manager's role is largely to do with managing change, then
what sorts of resistance is he likely to encounter?

Habit

You know from your own experience that habits are hard to break,
but the world of work is full of routines and habits. Salesmen need
to prepare their presentations when receiving new products but
need to be careful that the new form of presentation does not
become a habit. Have you met the salesman who has only one way
of presenting his product and despite all your attempts to tell him
that you're not interested, or you haven't got time, or your problem
is different, still starts at the beginning of his presentation and goes
through to the end without thinking?

Primacy

The way that people first cope with a situation may well establish a
persistent pattern. Research has shown that teachers, despite their
original training and further in-service training, often continue to
teach as they were taught. This pattern will often persist despite

conflicting information. People are very creative at producing self-fulfilling prophecies, remembering the instances when the preferred solution worked, and conveniently forgetting the occasions when it did not.

Self-interest

People will resist change if they feel they are losing something of value or increasing the chances of receiving something not wanted. Typically one of the losses that people fear is status. Another might be where a manager wants to increase the responsibility of his subordinate. In the manager's eyes this may be a benefit in that extra responsibility furthers his career, but to the subordinate it may be like an increase in the risk of failure. The important point to note is that where this occurs, people will concentrate on their own self-interests, irrespective of whether this coincides or conflicts with yours and the organisation's best interest.

Insecurity

Change will be resisted if the person feels he cannot cope or work in the new required way. This may go as far as feeling the job is at risk. This can and will happen when the individual rationally understands the need for the change, but emotionally cannot adjust to the new situation. Some subordinates will need support if they are going to cope with change.

Lack of trust

This is particularly important when you are in a new managerial situation. People will question your reasons for change and may lack your understanding of the situation. Is it being done for your ends or the company's? What commitment do you have to your subordinates? Do they believe you? You may need to do things that demonstrate that you can be trusted. You earn your right to trust by your actions, not by your words.

Differing perceptions

Your subordinates are unlikely to see the world in the way you do. For a start you are privy to information and views that they are not. You have different responsibilities, which means that the same data means something different to you. For instance, in a production packaging department for consumer goods, the volatile nature of the market means that there is a requirement for frequent changes in packaging materials. The manager may want to bring in more flexible machines and ways of working to meet these changing demands. To the line supervisors this may feel like accepting poor planning and making matters worse by agreeing to go along with it. Use your feedback skills to check if your perception matches your subordinates' views.

──────▶

HENRY BAKER – MANAGING CHANGE

This case looks at how to handle change in a young subordinate. A situation and the subordinate's behaviour is described, two different character studies are given, both consistent with the behaviour, and then ideas of how to manage the change are given.

The manager

You are the manager of an accounts department in a large company. You are about to see Henry Baker, one of your section managers, to undertake the annual appraisal. The details of the appraisal system are unimportant except that it reviews last year's performance, in order to improve work performance in the coming year. Henry, aged 25, qualified as an accountant three years ago. His present job is his first managerial/supervisory position and he was promoted to this position eighteen months ago. His department has about fifteen clerks working through three supervisors to him. You have thought about his work over the last twelve months and these are your conclusions.

Although he runs his department efficiently, his somewhat distant and dictatorial attitude to staff has created a great deal of underlying friction. For example, his insistence that all leave applications must be dealt with by him. He bypasses his supervisors frequently, dealing with the staff directly.

Through his work he has brought a substantial improvement in the credibility and reputation of your department. On his own initiative, he redesigned the monthly statements issued to the manufacturing departments on outputs and costs against budgets, and he ran seminars for the manufacturing managers on how to interpret and use these statements.

When he took over the department absenteeism and time-keeping were bad. They have now improved and this has led to a number of other tasks for management being undertaken. Although the amount of work being done by the department has increased, the overtime has been reduced, because of new working methods that Henry has introduced.

He has a tendency to retain routine managerial tasks himself, instead of delegating them to his supervisors. For instance, he personally controls absence and all overtime must be sanctioned by him.

His distant and at times arrogant manner has led to several disagreements with the union, who represent his clerks, and on one occasion only your intervention prevented a dispute from occurring.

Your general conclusion is that it has been a good year. The increasing quantity and quality of work his department has produced has exceeded your expectations. However, in the coming year he must do something about his manner and way of handling people, especially where the union is involved. Also he must start to delegate appropriate work to his supervisors.

*   *   *   *

Henry Baker type 1

Henry is a very ambitious man. He has great confidence in his ability, too much in fact, and he has justifiably been accused at times of being arrogant. However, there is no doubting his potential or his ability. Because of his drive he wants to introduce new ideas and seek improvements, frequently at a faster rate than his staff or supervisors can cope with. Coupled with this he hates mistakes and has tended, therefore, not to delegate, as in this way he ensures the job is done correctly and quickly. He feels the quantity and quality of work in his whole department reflects on him and, therefore, any way that gets the best results will get him the recognition that leads to promotion.

Henry Baker type 2

Technically, Henry is a first-class accountant and is always interested in keeping abreast of new developments in his field. He is a perfectionist and needs to feel totally certain before reaching an opinion. He is a shy man, who gives you the impression that he would rather deal with his figures than with people. Figures are predictable and can be manipulated; people are unpredictable, and this unnerves him. He is also very conscious that this is his first managerial position and that he is on trial. He feels the quantity and quality of the work of his whole department reflects on him. He is aware of his perfectionism and his desire to be seen to be doing a good job, and that at times he has insisted on work being done his way, and he feels his staff have seen this as being pedantic. This has reinforced his uncertainty about what his staff feel and how they will react, and he knows he has coped with this by doing jobs himself rather than delegating, as he should. It also avoids the situation where his subordinates might do the work in ways and at a standard that he would not accept, hence creating conflict. He dislikes conflict, always dealing with it by the rational approach, 'the figures show ...', but this does not seem to work too well with his staff. So this shy, uncertain man is seen by his staff as distant and unfeeling, and, as he is always technically correct, even arrogant at times.

How to get Henry to change

Let us take the example that in the coming year you want Henry to delegate routine activities to his supervisors. Taking Henry 1 to start with, what are likely to be his possible resistances to change? Certainly self-interest in that by doing the work himself he ensures effectiveness and, therefore, probably thinks it would in the end satisfy his career aspirations. Possibly also primacy: it works, it is no great effort, why change? Is there anything in the situation which is liable to make him change? Certainly his ambition and needs for high achievement and recognition could be used. If Henry could see a connection between satisfying his self-interest (ambition) and delegating, getting him to change should not be difficult. In other words, if Henry recognises that developing the skills of delegation would be a necessary requirement for higher-level jobs, he will delegate. This would need to be monitored and reinforced as he may change quickly, which would probably confuse his staff. It is also possible that under pressure and in crises he would revert to doing it himself.

This approach is unlikely to work with Henry 2. In fact it may make him feel even more insecure. Henry 2's major resistor would be insecurity. He already knows he should be delegating, but he is not sure how to, or whether he will cope. You will probably have to 'hold his hand'. Take a particular issue, such as overtime, work out with him how it should be controlled in future, how he should control his supervisor in this area and so on. The important point is that you would need to support him all through this change, taking it step by step, as this is the way Henry 2 will learn. He will not take risks knowingly, he will only go forward, when he is sure and feels safe to continue.

Let's take a second area of change — Henry's relationship with the union, particularly the incident when the manager had to intervene to prevent a dispute. Assume that both Henrys were upset by your intervention. Henry 1 reckons you overreacted and should have called the union's bluff; they would have backed off and there would not have been a dispute. Henry 2 believes the disagreement was over an important matter of principle, that your intervention led to an unsatisfactory compromise, and that his ideas will have to be implemented in the end.

How would you handle this issue with both Henrys? Remember in the same interview you will be raising the issue of him bypassing his supervisors and intervening with their staff.

1 *What do you think is the nature of the resistance for the two Henrys?*
2. *Are there any forces to help initiate the change for Henry 1 and for Henry 2?*
3. *How should the issue be raised with them?*
4. *What support or reinforcement will be needed?*

$$\longrightarrow$$

STRATEGIES FOR OVERCOMING RESISTANCE

Given that these are some of the resistances that managers introducing change are likely to encounter, what can be done to overcome them? What factors exist in the situation that may be used as a positive stimulus to change?

There tends to be an appropriate strategy to overcome the different resistances to change:

Negotiate

When the resistance stems from self-interest the best approach is to negotiate. Of course you are not negotiating about whether the change will happen, but negotiating or identifying possible advantages or incentives in the new situation, which will compensate for the perceived losses involved in the change.

Educate

Misunderstandings or lack of trust generate a range of worries and concerns about life after the change. If this is the case the best strategy is to educate, developing an understanding of the reasons for the change and its benefits.

Participate

When differing perceptions exist, participation can be used to involve the resisters and hence overcome the problems of change. Participation not only has the advantage of overcoming resistance, but because it introduces different people into the change process, with differing perceptions, information and ideas, better solutions are developed with a corresponding increase in commitment to them. Most people can remember an instance when, given a new product to make or a new way of working, they encountered a problem: a problem that was wholly predictable if only they had been asked.

Force and support

When people feel insecure or have worries about whether they will be able to cope, then force and support is an appropriate strategy. This seems to break the chain: I can't cope, I must be inadequate and I am afraid, change must be resisted. It works on the assumption that the imagined fears of the change are in fact greater than the actuality. The change is therefore implemented, the new behaviours supported and reinforced, generating feelings of 'this is not so bad as I imagined', leading to increased confidence.

This approach can also be used when the resistance stems from primacy or habit, although after the implementation other resistances may be encountered.

STRATEGY STYLE AND ROLE

In our model of interviewing, one of the key components is to establish the right role for the purpose and the outcome of the interview. Clearly the different strategies to overcome resistance will affect the outcomes from interviews. For example, if education is the appropriate strategy, then the manager will be clear about what he is trying to get his subordinates to understand. On the other hand, if participation is required, he may, at the start, be unsure or unaware of all the relevant issues. What relationships are appropriate for the various strategies?

Peter Honey and Graham Robinson in their work for the Bank of England and the British Civil Service maintain that it is vital to choose an appropriate style for each change strategy. We feel that it is more than style that must be appropriate. The difference in relationship, for instance, between a manager negotiating with a subordinate and a manager educating a member of his staff, is more than style. It also relates to the freedom and power of the individuals concerned, who has control and over what, who initiates and finishes the exchange, and so on. In other words the relationships are fundamentally different. However, Honey and Robinson's ideas are important and useful. It is for this reason that we mention them now.

While we concentrate on role rather than style, we do agree that the behaviours have to match the intentions and, therefore, specific roles must be established, if the change strategies are to have any hope of success.

Let's consider the case of Henry Baker, discussed earlier in this chapter, and apply the ideas about strategy and roles.

With Henry 1 his resistance to delegating was self-interest. Negotiation would appear to be the correct strategy. This would require an advisory role to get Henry to recognise that it is a skill he needs to develop to further his career. Then you would adopt a consultative role to negotiate new areas of work for Henry, which would mean he would have to delegate, in order to create the time to undertake new work.

The resistance of Henry 2 was insecurity, and a force and support strategy would be appropriate. This would require an executive role to inform him that he will delegate in future. Supporting Henry in this change could require an executive role to tell him how to delegate or a tutorial role to help him work out how he is going to manage.

OTHER FACTORS IN MANAGING CHANGE

Change is constantly going on all around us, so not all can be resisted. What factors encourage individuals to welcome change?

There are five styles to choose from:

→ Increasing Resistors Involvement
→ Increasing Initiators Involvement

Directing	Supporting	Consulting	Collaborating	Delegating
'I decide what changes are necessary and explain them.'	'I decide what changes I want to reinforce.'	'I explain the situation, invite ideas and then decide what to change.'	'I explain the situation, invite ideas and together we decide.'	'I explain the constraints and give authority to decide.'

If the preferred strategy is to negotiate then a collaborative style is best for resulting in agreement.

If the preferred change strategy is to educate, then the style depends on whether this is done by simply telling people or by helping them to discover for themselves the need for change. If time is short then education by telling may be necessary, in which case the directive style is the best fit. If there is a longer period for the educational process, then the consultative style is best.

If the preferred change strategy is one of participation and involvement, then the consultative or collaborative or delegative styles are appropriate, depending on the extent to which the manager initiating change feels 'safe' in relinquishing control.

Finally, if the preferred change strategy is force and support then a combination of the directive and supportive styles is the best fit.

Long ago, in *The Motivation to Work*, Herzberg identified *achievement* as one of the key motivators of managers. Change provides managers with new *challenges* and the possibility for new *achievements*. In turn this can bring new *rewards, status* and *career* opportunities. We have worked in several high-technology development environments, where the employees view new challenges as essential. For them the ability to keep abreast of new technologies and their implementation is essential to their career. Without this constant development of their capabilities, they see themselves being out of touch and their career adversely affected, both within the company and within the total labour market.

Always look for the positive motivations, which people bring into change situations. If someone is motivated by new achievements, it is much easier to build on this influence than to push to overcome any resistance he may have. It will also help to clarify the outcome of an interview in specific terms and to define the manager's role in relation to that outcome.

HOW PEOPLE CHANGE

People do not change overnight or immediately. Change in organisations or people is not like flicking a light switch. It is not only that people change gradually, but that new ideas or ways of working have to be integrated with the old ways. We are not talking about *everything* changing or being substituted – that is brainwashing. In a change process it is as important to identify and articulate what is *not* changing as well as what is. In our experience this frequently does not happen, and resistance is reinforced by managers announcing a change and creating the feeling that everything is new and strange. In consequence, they are seen to be threatening the relevance of the skills people already possess.

We work in a company which is experiencing rapid change in its products, its competitors and its markets. The company tries hard to communicate this and its consequences to its staff. The problem comes when the message indicating the changes in the business situation bears little direct relevance to shop-floor operatives or supervisors. They understand the importance and the need to change, but not what to change. What can an operator do about increasing competition?

These changes need translating into issues they can manage or affect. In fact, when this is done, a lot of higher-level change may not mean a significant change at all for lower levels. For example, unpredictability in the market-place often leads to lower stock levels, shorter production runs and more frequent and unplanned production changes from product to product. But the supervisor has always managed manufacturing changes, so the difference is an increasing frequency of a task he has done for years – inconvenient perhaps, but not unmanageable.

This is an oversimplified example. The important point is that a significant change in one part of the organisation, requiring new methods, concepts or ways of working, may in another part only require an increase in established practices. Similarly this idea is applicable if one considers jobs. Take the previous example of Henry Baker. His manager wants Henry to delegate certain tasks to his subordinates, but this is not his complete job. Large parts of his job will remain unchanged, and his manager will continue to want those tasks performed as he did in the past.

Another point about how individuals change and gradually adjust to new circumstances is that the ideas and new ways need to be constantly reinforced. In our experience, people can be classified into two basic types with regard to acceptance of change. There are people who change incrementally, and there are those who make an initial breakthrough and then often regress. We know people whom we have to take through changes step by step. They need to be clear and to understand before they go on to the next stage. This is not a matter of intelligence but the way they integrate new ideas or knowledge. We also know of people who return from a training course 'new men', but who forget it all within two weeks (see the diagram).

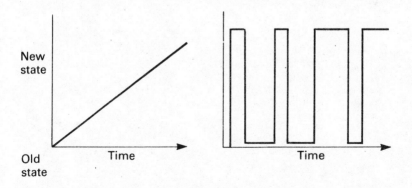

Both types clearly need reinforcing if the change is to stick. With one the manager may have to break the change down into steps that the person can assimilate and cope with. This approach would seem patronising for the other type, who would need to be presented with the lot, but then constantly reminded that he had forgotten and reverted to his old ways of working. This understanding helps to define the outcome of the interview, to choose an appropriate strategy for influencing the other person and ensuring that the role is appropriate.

SUMMARY

- Be sure what change you want to bring about. What is *not* changing?
- Define the changes in terms which relate to the other person's job.
- You know your own staff. Will they resist parts or all of the change? Identify the nature of the resistance. Identify any factors in the situation which will mean that the change will be welcomed.
- Choose a strategy to overcome the resistances and use the positives in the situation. Make sure the style and role are consistent with that strategy.
- Take into account the way people change. Are they 'incrementalists' or 'breakthrough' people? How will this affect the outcomes from the interviews that will be carried out?
- Be as patient as the circumstances allow!

Think about a change you are trying to introduce and apply these points to different people in your organisation.

CHAPTER NINE

Handling Redundancy

Redundancy has become a regular feature of many managers' lives, through having to handle the problem of making people redundant, and indeed being made redundant themselves. When we started working, the assumption was that people could join an organisation and stay there for the rest of their career. Training and career development schemes were often built on that assumption. It was even considered disloyal to think of leaving. One of our bosses refused to have any friendly conversation with anyone who tendered their resignation, even when it followed ten or more years with the company. We were told that if we stayed with our companies for the first six months we would probably be set for a lifetime career.

Of course that attitude has gradually changed over the past twenty years, in some cases dramatically. Even jobs which were seen as totally secure have become vulnerable, and the complete closure of factories and offices has not been restricted to the traditional industries. Many high-technology companies have been unable to survive in conditions of fierce competition.

The reasons for this have been explored in many other books and we will not repeat them. What is significant is that, despite all the changes and the ever-present redundancy announcements, managers still find redundancy as difficult and unpleasant as ever, and people still work with the assumption that their job is safe. 'Redundancy will not happen to me.'

Many managers seem to hold this same belief about job security, and perhaps it is important to maintain a positive attitude towards the continuity of work and employment. After all, without a sense of security many decisions concerning the future would never be taken. The problem is that holding these beliefs does not make it easy for managers to make people redundant. We still have managers on our courses who cannot, even in the role-play situation, get the word 'redundant' out, and who go all round the subject without being able to say it.

Our model of interviewing helps us to understand why the

interview, or interviews associated with redundancy are difficult. If the manager holds some of these values about work, and expects that the person being made redundant does too, this puts him under considerable pressure. If it is someone they have known for some time, their relationship as people can become confused with their relationship in work roles. Perhaps more than in any other interview the manager is the representative of the company. A decision will often have been taken at a senior level that there must be a 10 per cent cut, and it does not matter if individual managers agree or not, they still have to carry them out. This in itself can make it difficult, especially if the manager does not agree with the decision.

The manager will often expect the other person to react emotionally, indeed to 'attack' them personally. It will feel as if the interview cannot be planned, because it is not possible to predict the reactions of the other person. There will often be a pressure felt from the other subordinates. If they are not being made redundant, they may feel relieved, but they will be very interested in how the process is being carried out. The boss may feel that he or she is on trial. These and other pressures, will often mean that while the boss is very clear what the purpose of the interview is, the situation can be very 'de-skilling' and the outcome may shift.

BE CLEAR ABOUT THE REQUIRED OUTCOME

The outcome you can achieve will, of course, depend on the circumstances, the company policy, and the person involved, but in general there are several stages to the redundancy process. In terms of conducting the interviews successfully, they do not all have to be achieved at once. Indeed it is often the role of the manager to announce the redundancy, and then to set up relationships to deal with other matters, rather than dealing with everything at once. If we assume that the subordinate has not been prepared for redundancy, and that it is not something they want, there are likely to be the following steps in the process:

- Announcing that the person will be made redundant
- Giving the person the opportunity to 'react'
- Telling them about the 'terms and conditions'
- Helping them to leave.

Other tasks may be undertaken by the company which will broaden the purpose of the interview, and will change the desired outcome, such as,

- Finding out how the redundancy will affect them
- Providing support through the psychological adjustment
- Providing support for the material adjustment
- Providing assistance with re-employment.

Not all these steps are provided by all organisations, and some are provided by specialist personnel, or sub-contracted to counselling services. What is clear from our experience is that often the manager will try to do too much in the initial interview. The purpose can then become very confused if they try to be boss, information-giver, counsellor and supporter all at the same time. Often, they are not very successful at any of them.

It may well be that for some subordinates the only achievable outcome is that they will understand that they are being made redundant. If the manager goes on to explain the terms and conditions, it may help the manager feel better that the company is being very generous and giving all this help, but if the subordinate is feeling very upset he may only partly hear what is being said, or may not hear at all. Even worse, he may feel that the boss and indeed the company is not even prepared to listen to his feelings of hurt and worry. The result may be that there is a total rejection of the manager. As we said earlier, other employees will be watching how the interviews are being handled. They may only see the apparent lack of concern by management, and this may affect them, even the ones who are not made redundant. All this begins to suggest certain strategies for conducting the interview, and we will return to this later.

Managing feelings by understanding them

The reason that many managers do not handle redundancy well is that their feelings of not wanting to conduct the interview(s) cloud their judgements. Understanding what happens, and why, can be a way of managing those feelings, and then the interviews.

Understanding reactions to redundancy

As we mentioned above, research into the effects of unemployment started in the 1930s depression, both in Europe and the USA, and many more recent studies have produced remarkably similar results, even in different countries with varied economic circumstances.

There are a number of phases which people seem to go through. The first is one of disbelief or shock. Even if there is an awareness of the state of the business or rumours of job losses, there still seems to be difficulty accepting that 'it could happen to me'. This stage tends to be short, up to a week, and sometimes there is a dramatic change overnight.

The next phase is characterised by denial or optimism. There is little worry about the future, and the situation is considered as temporary. Sometimes this is expressed as 'time off' which has been earned for hard work.

The third phase is characterised by increased anxiety and distress. Most people, when confronted with continuing evidence of a change in reality, come to realise that they will have to make changes to their way of living. At this stage they may become depressed, because although they realise changes will have to be made, they do not want or know how to make these changes. Previous employment can be idealised, and the negatives disguised. Hopes of finding a job begin to fade, and the unemployed identity is gradually assumed. This stage can last for months.

Gradually the person will move into the last phase of acceptance of the new reality, releasing themselves from the assumptions of the previous employment, and settling down to a new way of life with different standards and expectations.

These responses of shock, denial and optimism, anxiety and depression, and finally adaptation or resignation may be recognised by some of you as the normal phases of mourning. Just as in mourning the dead, these phases are sometimes in the open for all to see, and in other cases they are covered by a veneer of 'normal living'. Understanding that they are normal may help the manager dealing with redundancy at work. You cannot expect someone to move directly to acceptance, or if they do the other phases are likely to come later. Some writers see these phases as quite normal in all processes of major change, where the change is particularly significant and difficult for the person concerned. Try to use the ideas to help you prepare emotionally for the interview. You will see in the transcript of a redundancy interview later in the chapter that shock and denial create problems for the manager, but if you know they are normal reactions it should make it easier to accept them, and not let them push you away from what you are trying to achieve. The shock and denial, if it is stronger than you had predicted, may mean that you cannot achieve as much as you had planned, and you will have to modify your approach.

We have included here some theory about the meaning of work, because we think that if managers can understand what redundancy may be threatening or taking away from people, it may be possible to cope with the feelings more effectively. It may also help the manager understand why the person who is being made redundant can say things which do not seem to be immediately relevant, and which can be very hurtful, especially if you have given considerable thought and care to the way you tell them.

You will have to decide for the people you are dealing with, from your own knowledge of them, what redundancy will mean to them, but be careful not to assume that everyone else thinks and feels as you do.

THEORIES ABOUT THE MEANING OF WORK

Work is a source of income

For many people this is the assumption or the explicit reason for work. Of course most people do need the income, and often this is a prime worry for people made redundant. In many cases the company provisions do at least buffer this worry for some time. It is surprising though that even people who win very large sums of money, for example in lotteries, often continue to work, or after a short break seek new employment. We, therefore, cannot assume that this is the only concern.

Work is a source of activity

The disabled give as a reason for wanting to work that they wish to alleviate their chronic boredom and inactivity. People who complain about having to work, often find when they are forced not to work, that they need the activity. For many who are made redundant, a first reaction is 'What will I do with myself?'

Work provides relationships outside the family

The classic Herzberg studies found that the most frequently mentioned satisfaction from work was 'social aspects of the job'. In an urban setting, in particular, the unemployed suffer from social isolation, and the balance of family relationships is often maintained by the emotional outlets at work.

Work structures time

It determines when to get up, when to leave home, and how

time is spent at work. It differentiates weekdays from week-
ends, and holidays from working days.

Work is a source of creativity and skill

Work provides the opportunity to develop skills and to be
valued for them. Craftsmen are often very proud of their skills,
but they do not have much value without work. Creativity
means that people can feel that they have achieved something,
that they have mastered some new activity, and without work
that satisfaction can be taken away.

Work gives a sense of purpose

Work is for many people the only connection they have to the
community in terms of offering or contributing to something
that is useful.

Work gives people identity

In modern society work roles are often the most important
sources of identity. A doctor is known as such not just by their
patients, but also by friends and neighbours. These people are
able to make assumptions about their background, education,
income, style of living and so on. It gives them a status in
society, but this is also conferred on the whole family. Unemployment can remove all that. Argyris sees personal development as a growth from total dependence at birth towards
independence. Enforced dependence, through redundancy,
will often produce in mature people feelings of failure, as
though they are somehow disgraced in the eyes of their family
and others. There have been cases of people hiding it from
their families, to the extent of going out of the home at the
same time as normal, even when they no longer have a job.

Most people will have a complex set of reasons for working,
probably a combination of those outlined above. Thinking about
the individual you are going to make redundant may help you to
find appropriate ways of linking it to what is important to them, and
recognising, for example, what they will miss. It may also help you
to listen to what they say, and understand some of the things that
are said. You may get information, or clues as to the kind of help

they may need, and the problems they are going to have coping with redundancy. It is quite likely that they will not have articulated the functions and values of work even to themselves, until they are faced with the prospect of not having it. A successful redundancy interview may move from announcing the fact, often using words that acknowledge what the person will miss, to listening to what they have to say, because you may be wrong in your assumptions, and as they struggle to articulate the loss you may learn things that will be useful later. Above all, do not assume that your reasons for working are shared by everyone else!

POSITIVE ATTITUDES TO REDUNDANCY

The phases of redundancy seem to be a normal process of change when people suffer great loss. But for some people their identity is not threatened, their attitude to the job loss may be positive, and consequently their reactions may be different. What factors may mean the phases are changed?

Financial security

This may mean that the person feels able to maintain their life-style for the time being, and to hold on to many of the assumptions about themselves. Severance pay may provide this for some people, but if the unemployment is long the same phases of change and loss may just be delayed.

Legitimate unemployment

This is where people can go through the change without their self-esteem being threatened, because they think, and others believe, that the change from work to non-work was legitimate. They personally are not to blame. If they are genuinely offered early retirement, or where a whole factory or organisation closes, it is much easier to see this as legitimate unemployment. Of course, that form of coping may be very temporary. If they need companionship, sense of purpose, structuring of time, and recognition of skill, knowing that it was not their fault may not be helpful for very long.

Professional orientation

When some professionals see their career as more important than a job, they can rationalise redundancy as a 'break' in their career. This can be reinforced if there is normally a great deal of mobility between organisations, and the individual's attachment to a particular organisation is low. Some people enjoy setting up projects, and when the project finishes, it provides the opportunity to move on and start another one.

Social support

This is when people are able to retain membership of their preredundancy work group, for example where everyone is made redundant, and they can still associate together for social support and companionship. Sometimes these situations will last long after the employment has gone. In mining villages the miners' clubs can provide the social setting for that support, and the identity and status patterns which existed in work will often be carried for years in the clubs.

Alternative work

Education, training, or voluntary work may alleviate boredom, and in terms of self and public perception symbolise a willingness to work and, therefore, reduce the stigma of the unemployed, the idea that they are lazy.

IT'S WORSE FOR THE VERY AMBITIOUS

The factors listed above are likely to soften the effect of the change generally, but for the high achiever who has been successful in fulfilling ambitions at work, the phases may be experienced with increased intensity. The particularly ambitious person may invest large parts of their time and energy in work, and the product of that investment will be important in maintaining their self-image. Success at work means that the self-image is reinforced and becomes a central and important part of the self. For them the loss of work, which has become so important, can be particularly traumatic. The loss of the work role requires fundamental adjustments of their assumptions about themselves, and this can mean extreme behaviour in each of the phases. Seligman (1975) outlines a typical case:

Recently, a 42-year-old business executive, temporarily unemployed, came to see me for some vocational advice. Actually, it was his wife who first contacted me; having read a popular article of mine on helplessness, she asked me to talk with her husband, Mel, because he looked helpless to her. For the last twenty years Mel had been a rising executive. Until a year ago he had been in charge of production for a multi-million-dollar company involved in the space programme. When the government decreased its financial support for space research, he lost his job, and was forced to take a new executive position in another city, in a company he described as 'back-biting'. After six miserable months he quit. For a month he sat listlessly around the house, and made no effort to find work; the slightest annoyance drove him into a rage of anger; he was unsocial and withdrawn. Finally his wife prevailed on Mel to take some vocational guidance tests that might help him find a satisfying job.

When the results of these tests came back, they revealed that he had a low tolerance for frustration, that he was unsociable, that he was incapable of taking responsibility, and that routine prescribed work best fitted his personality. The vocational guidance company recommended that he became a worker on an assembly line. This advice came as a shock to Mel and his wife, since he had twenty years of high executive achievement behind him, was usually outgoing and persuasive, and was much brighter than most sewing machine operators. But these tests actually reflected his present state of mind: he believed every small obstacle was insurmountable, he was not interested in other people, and he could barely force himself to get dressed, much less make important career decisions. But this profile did not give a true picture of Mel's character; rather it reflected a process, probably temporary, that had been going on since he lost his job – the disorder of depression.

MANAGING REDUNDANCY INTERVIEWS

The key issue in conducting successful redundancy interviews is managing your own feelings. We have been over some of the key ideas and theories connected with redundancy in the hope that the understanding will help you manage those feelings more successfully.

From your point of view you may have considered all manner of options before deciding to make a particular person redundant. You may have agonised over the decision and feel that in the end it is the only possible decision that could be made, but from the other person's emotional standpoint the decision will not be right. It will not feel fair, and the grounds that you think are reasonable will probably seem quite unreasonable to them.

Given the phases which people go through, they are likely to be shocked, and to disbelieve what you are saying. Certainly once they understand that you are making them redundant, their 'desired outcome' is likely to be to show that you have made a mistake, or simply not to accept it and to take it to another, or higher, authority. If they are frightened of all the pressures and influences which suddenly will seem very real – the loss of income, what they are going to do, the loss of social contacts, the loss of sense of purpose, the devaluing of their skills, and how they are going to face their family and friends – they may feel very angry, and want to hit out at the person who is giving them all this pain. If that is the case, they may say all sorts of things that are meant to hurt and put some pressure on you. These may not be rational, and are likely to include things from the history of the relationship. They may include emotional appeals: 'George, we have worked together for over ten years ...' The temptation for the manager will be to answer the criticisms, and to defend the action. The purpose will be lost and the outcome is quite likely to be an argument.

Some people's hurt and anger will be contained. The value that authority should not be challenged may be important even in these circumstances, and they may lapse into angry frustrated silence. For many managers this can be as bad or worse, because there is no feedback. Under these circumstances we find that the manager will often go on talking, just to fill the silence, covering all the issues about the redundancy, even when they know that the person is probably not listening. They may even make offers of help which are quite inappropriate for the other person's needs, but the talking keeps the interview going.

The other common pitfall is that the manager knows that the person being made redundant is likely to get angry, so that they try to control the interview inappropriately. Remember you do not lose control by giving the other person the chance to express their feelings. They will 'run out of steam', and if you listen attentively at least you are expressing your interest. You can only control the interview by picking up only those issues which help you achieve your purpose. Inappropriate control often means the manager talking too much, not listening to what is said, guessing what the reaction will be and providing answers. Typically this will come out as if the manager is trying to 'sell' the advantages of redundancy. Is it possible for someone to buy, when they are frightened of all the pressures?

------------▶

A CLERICAL REDUNDANCY

You are the manager of a department in which there are a large number of clerical and administrative staff providing a service to the line management. As a result of general business difficulties, there have been staff reductions in a number of line activities, which are now affecting your ability to support your present staffing levels.

You need to reduce the department by ten people and you have some flexibility about the timing, although the reduction must be completed within six months. There are three staff due to retire in the coming year, and they have volunteered for redundancy. You had hoped to find another seven staff interested in voluntary redundancy, but in the end were faced with the problem of selecting two members of the department.

Currently, there are three trainees in the department, all about to finish their basic training periods. The feeling of many of the staff is that two of the trainees should be made redundant rather than the more experienced members of staff. You are prepared to make one of the trainees redundant, since his performance has been below standard for the last nine months and he has not been able to improve it. However, the other two have both had excellent reports and have potential to become very useful members of the department. You have, therefore, decided that you will retain both and make one of the clerical staff redundant, because he has had a persistently poor performance and absence record since joining the department about two years ago.

He moved into your department when he was made 'surplus to requirements' in his previous department, where his work performance was not very good – as you discovered after you had agreed to take him. He has had more than an average amount of time off for sickness. How much is genuinely due to his bronchial complaint and how much is due to an arrangement with his doctor, you do not know. His time off for sickness is, however, decreasing. You have warned him about his poor performance twice in the last three months. He has ten years service, in total, with the company.

$\longrightarrow$

Using the model to plan the interview

What is the purpose of the interview, and what outcomes do you want to achieve from this first interview?

The purpose is to make the man redundant in a way which will be responsible within the company culture, and which will not cause any problems with the staff who will remain. There might be other considerations in your particular place of work, but this thinking sets the interview in its context.

There are choices about the specific outcome that you want to achieve in the first interview. The least you will want to achieve is that he leaves the interview knowing that he is being made redundant.

If we assume that you do not know this man very well, you may not be sure what effect the redundancy will have, but you do know that he has been away ill a lot and that you have spoken to him about this and his performance. He is quite likely to feel that the decision is very unfair. The other staff are expecting the trainees to go first, and he will probably be expecting the same. We can, therefore, assume that the interview will come as something of a shock to him and possibly to the other staff. It will, therefore, be important to conduct it in a way that demonstrates, at least to the other staff, that you are handling it reasonably and giving him a fair hearing. This may change your outcome to ensuring that he understands that he is going to be made redundant, giving him the opportunity to react and tell you about his worries, and assuring him that the company will support his efforts to get another job. You may also like to have in reserve the outcome that you will start the process of finding out about how the redundancy will affect him, and assuring him that you will notify him very quickly about the terms and conditions of the redundancy. But remember the research about redundancy, and our assumption that he is likely to be shocked at your decision because he will be expecting a trainee to go. In this condition will he really be able to tell you rationally how it will affect him? Will he be in a suitable frame of mind to listen to the terms and conditions? Remember the purpose is not to make you feel better!

Detailed advance planning

The first part of the interview needs to be planned in detail. Many people, even very experienced managers, write out the words they are going to use in a redundancy interview. It is so easy to let the odd word slip in when you are feeling uncomfortable, and the odd word can turn a managed interview into chaos very quickly when feelings are running high. There are no easy ways to tell someone that they are going to be made redundant. You may as well be straightforward and say what you mean. From your point of view it may feel brutally frank, but it can be very confusing if you start talking about the state of the economy, the company's capital investment programme and the difficulties that you have had coming to a decision. It may need enough explanation to demonstrate

that there was some thought, but do not forget that he will probably not accept your rationale anyway.

What role is appropriate?

For the first part you must be in the executive role. You are the boss.
You must appear as if you are responsible for the decision, and that
it is certainly not up for discussion. Later parts of the process may
well mean that you have to be adviser, counsellor, information
provider and so on. This is another reason for not trying to do too
much in the first interview, because it will mean that you have to
switch roles, and as we said earlier, this will make the interview
more complex.

If you have decided that you will also give him a chance to react,
so that he feels he has had a fair hearing, do not be seduced into
being the counsellor at this stage. You are still in the executive role,
but the concerned boss listening to what is being said. You may
well get all sorts of clues which will help you plan later parts of the
process, or you may find that it has all changed the next day when
he has talked to his family. This is a good example of where you
remain in the same role – executive – but the style changes from
formal announcer to caring listener.

What pressures and influences may there be?

Remember that he does not know why you want to see him. He is
expecting the trainees to be made redundant, so there is no reason
why he should be coming in aggressively. All the pressures on him
– concern about his family, his status, money, and so on – will begin
to build once you have told him, but before the interview they are
all in your mind not his.

Initially most of the pressures are on the manager. There may be
guilt about having to deprive someone of their living. There may be
the other staff and how they will react. There may be the boss and
being seen to do the job effectively. There may be the unions and
how they will react, and so on. This is why you have to be clearly in
the executive role. Plan out what you are going to say and structure
the interview, so that you can manage these pressures on you.

What skills will you need?

The first part of the interview is presenting the information. This
will not take very long. It depends who it is, how much explanation

is required, but there will probably be no need to explain the purpose of the interview. The information will need to be sequenced to give explanation for the decision, but very briefly; only one idea should be introduced at a time, and the first phase should finish with a brief summary. The only feedback skill will be identifying the extent to which the words are understood.

In the second part of the interview – giving the person the opportunity to react – the required skills are eliciting rather than presenting. Because you may well be attacked, and because of the pressures you feel, you will want to justify or explain further, but the desired outcome now is that he feels he has had a chance to tell you. You need to listen, but in an active way. You should encourage him to talk with supporting statements, demonstrate that you are listening by using his words to frame any questions and summaries.

You will manage the potentially difficult emotions by setting the right climate. It will be helpful to both of you if the interview is conducted formally and kept at the formal level. It may well be that this person's absences have created problems for you in the past, but do not let those feelings show. If you are feeling guilty or uncomfortable about having to conduct the interview, do not make emotional appeals to him to feel sorry for you. 'You must see how difficult this is for me,' is not an unusual phrase in the circumstances, but it almost always leads to a discussion about who has the most difficult problem to deal with and the interviewee will win that argument.

How will the interview go?

This transcript is of an actual interview, and as you will see it is not meant to be an example of 'how to do it', but illustrative of some of the things that can happen. We have deliberately not edited the transcript, so that you can see some real examples of the things we have talked about.

Manager: Good morning, John. Would you like to take a seat.

The opening is appropriately formal and polite.

John: Thank you.
M: Obviously you don't know why I've asked you to come in to see me today.

This next comment immediately risks giving control of the interview to the subordinate by inviting him to suggest why it is taking place. It is an illustration of how the discomfort of the situation makes the experienced manager ask a question, to test out what the subordinate already knows rather than getting on with the job. This is no place for a question.

J: Well yes I do, and I am so grateful to you, because I feel so much better now. I know that I've had these problems, but I am all right and well now. I had asked to see you because ...

The subordinate is then able to make the assumption that they are there to discuss his recent illness, and the purpose and the desired outcome have gone out of the window. If this does happen to you, just keep quiet until they have finished, say something polite like 'I understand that you would want to talk about that, but ...' and regain the control.

M: I didn't realise that you had asked to see me ...
J: Yes I had because I want to thank you, because you've been so patient with me. I know I've had a bit of time off, but if you think, I have worked here for ten years, and it's not very much. And as I say I'm all right now, and I want to thank you ...
M: I don't want to interrupt, but unfortunately I'm going to have to come in, if you wouldn't mind. I didn't know that you wanted to see me. I wanted to see you, but not about your sickness record, which has, in fact, been rather more than you say, but that is not the purpose of the interview.

Finally the manager does decide to interrupt. He makes it clear that the sickness record is not the reason for the interview, but then goes on to discuss it: 'it has, in fact, been rather more than you say.' Under the circumstances this is hardly relevant, but we often find that managers do not like to let a point of argument go, even if it is not relevant. Because the manager picks the sickness up, John continues to discuss it. After all his purpose for the interview is to explain to the manager that he is fit and well again now, and ready to get back to work. The opportunity for 'one of these little chats' is just right.

J: No. No. Well as I am better I am quite happy to take on more work, because I realise that the company needs ...
M: John, I know in the past we've had the chance to have little chats ...
J: Yes, yes.
M: But unfortunately on this occasion I have to interrupt you. You have heard ...
J: I don't understand you. What do you mean?

M: Well perhaps if you give me a chance to explain what I mean, you will.

J: Sorry.

The whole atmosphere is becoming far too informal, and it is not clear what role the manager is in. He is finally forced to become the 'punishing parent' to gain some control.

M: You've heard the rumours which have been going around. You've seen the redundancies which have taken place. I'm well aware that everybody's been talking about the situation. However I will clarify it for you.

J: I knew that some people were going early ...

M: The production line have been having a lot of problems. The business hasn't been doing very well and the central admin function have been asked to tighten their belt. What we have had to do, as you know ... the three on the file ledger, they've been retired early, at their own request and unfortunately what we have to do is rationalise the other people and see how we can cope with the work, bearing in mind that there's now going to be a shortage of work. (John interrupts the last few words)

J: I am happy to take on more work. As you know, in the past I have worked in the other departments, so one of the advantages of having been with the company some time is that I've got good all-round experience.

This part is much better, and should have been the beginning of the interview. There is only one thing to say in this interview to achieve the minimum outcome, but it feels a little more reasonable if some explanation is given. The interviewee will be listening at this point, and it may even make some sense once they have got over the shock. Here the manager is starting the explanation from the reasonable assumption that the employee may have heard rumours. The first interruption is appropriately ignored.

The explanation continues quite reasonably, but it is full of euphemisms, like 'tighten their belt', 'retired early' and 'rationalise the other people'. It is therefore not unrealistic that John gets the message that more work will be demanded of him, and under the circumstances he is very anxious to assure his boss that he is up to it.

M: What the ...

J: And I am grateful for the employment that the company has always given me. I am sorry that people have got to lose their jobs but ...

M: John, you're not listening to me. What I said was not that we have to take on more work but we are now in a situation where we will have *less* work. To cope with this situation, we are at present over-manned. We have had to look at what each member of the department provides, what part of the work they do and what can be easily absorbed into another member's work. And ...
J: I don't mind doing other people's work.

The manager would keep control by being more straightforward and, indeed, after the interruption is much more explicit – 'we are now in a situation where we have less work ...' but the sentence cannot quite be finished – '... and therefore the decision has reluctantly been made that you will be redundant.' It does seem harsh, but by going round the subject, the manager allows John 'not to hear'. He comes to the wrong conclusion yet again, and then has to be told about his redundancy in the context of offering to do more work. This section, however, is quite good and would have been a good start to the interview.

M: Unfortunately, John, you are one of the people chosen for redundancy.
J: That's unbelievable.
M: I can understand that it would feel like that to you. This is why I felt when you came in that you didn't understand, and I wanted to speak to you quickly, before you got hold of the wrong end of the stick.
(*long pause*)

The long pause at the end is a clear indication that the first desired outcome 'announcing that the person will be made redundant' has been achieved. The question the manager is facing now is whether to continue and try to achieve the other outcomes.

M: Would it help at all if I explained why? Or would you prefer time to think about it?
J: You said why.

This is the question which the manager poses to test out the employee's readiness to continue. The answer is a belligerent: 'You've already told me why.'

M: It is the fact that the part of the work you are doing is most easily absorbed into existing jobs. This has been looked at rationally, and not at all from a personal point of view, simply that the work you do is most easily absorbed into other people's jobs. I realise that this must be a personal shock ...

The manager goes on to try to be reassuring that the decision is not personal, but it should be clear that this will not be effective. It will feel personal.

J: Am I the only one to be made redundant?
M: No, all in all there were ten people. Which is why I said there had been rumours. I know people have been talking about it, and I thought perhaps you were aware.
J: Well I knew that there were some people taking early retirement.
M: There have been those three, and there have been five voluntary retirements, and there have to be another two. We have to have ten redundancies in order that we can continue to function.
J: Well how are the other two to be chosen?

The employee responds, however, by asking for reassurance that he is not the only one. The key thing for the manager to realise at this stage of shock is that most of what is being said will probably not be remembered, and the appropriate outcome is that they feel they have had the chance to react, and vent their feelings. There is a clue about denial in the phrase 'How are the other two to be chosen?'

M: What we had to do was look at the work that has to be done and it is not the person who is made redundant. I realise that it feels like that at the moment, but it is the work which you do which is the most easily absorbed.
J: Presumably, well I don't know anything about redundancy, but presumably you have selected people against length of service.

The manager responds by continuing with the reassurance, and the interview remains fairly calm at this point. The question from the employee about selecting people according to length of service is another attempt to be reassured that the decision was 'procedural', and not personal.

M: No. Our company policy is not to go purely on length of service. What we have to do is look at the skills in the department, which skills we need to keep us going, and which we can manage without. In your case, particularly, it was not so much the skills as the actual job that is done.
J: That doesn't make sense. You just said skills and I've got the skills to do any of the other jobs. I've been in all the other departments.

The manager feels, however, here is something which can be dealt with in terms of explanation of policy.
The feedback is that it was the wrong response. All the employee wants is to be told that he is all right, and that his skills are valuable.

M: When you look at selection for redundancy ...
J: This sounds very, very fishy.
M: We look at two areas ...
J: You said you look at skills. I've got more skills than all the others rolled into one, and I probably should have your job.
M: Can I explain?
J: No, you're talking rubbish.
M: I said we look at two areas ...
J: You're just changing your story. You told me ...
M: No. What I said is that we look at the work that you do, and that work can be most easily absorbed.
J: I can do everyone's work, and yours!
M: Unfortunately when we looked at the work load, it would appear that the work you do ...
J: I think it's disgraceful! You got me in here by myself. I had no knowledge. Surely I'm entitled to some sort of help and assistance. Am I able to appeal against this?
M: When you have perhaps calmed down a little ... I can understand you must feel very angry and very upset. What we do ...

The manager tries to complete the rational argument and justify the company decision. He needs to remember the outcome that he is supposed to be achieving. The explanation of the decision should have been in the first part of the interview, and this part is for the employee to react. Now what happens is that every time the employee tries to react, the manager tries to give an explanation. What it feels like to the employee is that the manager is not listening, and is not interested in how it feels from his point of view. So it is not surprising that he gets angry, and starts to lash out at the person who has just hurt him: 'I probably should have your job,' and 'no, you're talking rubbish.'

The manager should be using the eliciting skills, listening and not being so anxious to control the interview. If the subordinate is to react to this awful news, he must be given the space to react.

The manager says, 'I can understand that you feel very angry and upset,' but the 'anger and upset' is almost as much about the way the interview is going as about the redundancy. On the one hand the manager is saying, 'I can understand that you must feel very angry', but on the other hand he wants him to calm down and stop showing that anger. It is our experience that if people in these circumstances are allowed to be angry' and to show it, the incident does not last very long. It also seems to us not unreasonable that they should be angry, or upset.

The problem is that the manager needs to control the feelings of
loss of control. Sitting back, listening, even asking questions will
perhaps encourage the release of the anger, but it will also give the
manager time to decide which items to pick up, which to ignore, and
which will be useful for later interviews.

J: More than upset. I'm totally shattered. What about my family?
What about my wife? What about my children? I've worked for the
company ten years. I've not been a well man, and now you treat me
like this. Other people have been with the company for three
months and you're continuing to employ them. What sort of
company is this? I shall go to the papers over this.
M: If you feel you must do these things ... What I can offer ... at the
moment it's natural that you are in a state of shock.
J: I'm not shocked. I'm quite calm.
M: These feelings appear to me to be perfectly natural. What we can
offer is a counselling service for you to talk about these things, and
about the effect that it will have on you ...
J: You what! I just want my job. I don't want a **** counsellor!

The next part begins with an angry, but also frightened outburst.
The manager picks up on the last point about going to the papers. It
would have been much more helpful to pick up on the family, and
build a link to the next point about the counselling service.

There is still this tendency for the manager to argue each point: 'It is
natural that you're in a state of shock.' 'I'm not shocked.' 'These
(shocked) feelings appear to me to be perfectly natural.' The counsellor is offered in the context of this argument, so it is not
surprising that the offer is rejected. This is not helpful for later
phases of the redundancy process, when the employee may need
help but not feel able to ask for it, having rejected it at this stage.
The manager should try to ensure that employees do not put
themselves in this position.

M: Unfortunately, if you've been selected for redundancy, there is
very little you can do about it.
J: I've got no rights. No appeal. No nothing. I've got nothing.
M: You are not being disciplined, John. This is a redundancy
situation. There isn't an appeal. Because the job is redundant. There
is nothing personal against you. Nothing to do with you.
J: That's rubbish. We have flexibility between jobs. I mean I have
been doing Fay's job for three weeks. She's not being made redun-

dant. I could do her job. I could do any job. I've done everything in
the whole ******* department. They brought me into your department. I'm paid more. I was promoted.
M: Well I think, obviously, in the mood you are in, which is quite
natural ...
J: I just feel ... I don't know what I'm saying. I don't know what I am
doing.

This is so typical of what happens when the manager is in the
arguing mode. Instead of picking up why the employee does not
want a counsellor, if anything needs to be picked up, the issue of
wanting the job back is discussed. We are now back to the first part
of the interview, the irrevocability of the decision, and the manager
took it there. It evokes the angry response: 'No right. No appeal. No
nothing.' The anger goes on until the rather pathetic, and perhaps
apologetic 'I just feel ... I don't know what I am saying. I don't know
what I am doing.'

M: I can understand that. Perhaps if you'll let me make a suggestion.
This is not the place for me to try and help you ...
J: You're not helping me.
M: You don't want my help.
J: Bloody right I don't.
M: I can say to you, if you will listen for a few minutes.
J: Listen to you? I've heard every word.
M: Your redundancy ...
J: I don't accept it.
M: What I am telling you, whether you are listening at this moment
or not, is that you will receive a very generous redundancy package.
J: You're not going to buy me off. You're taking away my living,
my respect ...
M: I'm sure that is how you feel. That is not ...
J: My career.
M: It is not the intention to take away your respect.
J: What treating me like this! Ten years service and then you throw
me out on the street. In front of people who have only been here
three weeks.
M: I cannot involve myself in this kind of argument.
J: I thought there had to be consultation about redundancies.
M: No. If you had not talked so much, I would perhaps have been
able to explain to you that you are entitled to three months notice,
or pay in lieu of notice. In our case because we are the kind of
company we are ...

J: I just want to stay.

The manager feels the need to help, and says so, but before the offer can come out it has been rejected. The manager does not control the feelings of rejection, and then is left with only the 'angry parent' role to try and regain control. It is not accepted this time, and it degenerates with the natural, but not very sensible phrase 'I am telling you, whether you are listening or not!' followed by 'I cannot involve myself in this kind of argument' and 'If you had not talked so much, I would perhaps have been able to explain ...'

In expressing his anger John uses many of the skills of interviewing. He uses the other person's words to demonstrate that he is listening; he uses the emotional appeals to change the atmosphere of the interview; he uses the eliciting skills to put pressure on the manager; and once he is clear what the purpose is, he directs the conversation towards anything but that, and he does it all without having to think twice.

M: You will have three months notice from when I formalise it, which will be from tomorrow, but you will also receive three months money in addition, because that is the company policy.

J: I want to work out my notice.

M: As I said, I don't want to get into details with the money. The personnel department will talk to you about your benefit.

J: So you are kicking me out and not even bothering to tell me what I'm entitled to.

M: Personnel department will do that.

J: You can't be bothered.

M: No, it's not that. I want you to have the fairest treatment that you can have ...

J: Well you're not treating me fairly.

M: The personnel department are the people who know the details of the scheme, and they're much better at that than I am. I want to make sure that you get everything that you're entitled to. They'll work on the facts and figures ...

J: Oh, human beings don't come into it!

M: Not for redundancy, and you might think that that is a bad thing, but they take your age, and length of service into account, and make sure you get your fullest entitlement.

J: I don't want to go.

M: I'm sure you don't, John, but I am afraid there isn't an alternative. We have looked at the alternatives, but because of the cutbacks there's nowhere else that we can use your services.

J: Why can't Theresa Mills go? She's not a suitable person. She's only been here three weeks.
M: The work that Theresa does is different to yours.
J: I could do it though, and I'm quite prepared to do it.
M: You may well think that you can do it, but that is not the decision, and I am not prepared to discuss what Theresa does.

As the interview becomes less and less successful, the manager changes outcome again, and begins to explain the terms and conditions of the redundancy, but does not have all the facts to do it. The risk is clear from what happens. It appears that the manager cannot even be bothered to find out the facts, although the strategy of letting the personnel department deal with the complex detail may well have been a sensible one. Such information cannot be handled very well in the middle of an argument. As a general rule, arguments are not very useful to managers in these kind of interviews. They should be avoided.

———————————————➤

CHAPTER TEN

Effective Appraisals

In this chapter we are going to consider the appraisal interview from three standpoints:

- the reasons why organisations have appraisal schemes and the effect these have on the interview,
- the key issues and factors that the manager must get right to achieve effective appraisals,
- how to manage the appraisal interview.

Appraisal Schemes: purposes and problems

In a recent survey of UK companies, carried out for the Institute of Personnel Management, 82 per cent of companies interviewed operated a performance review scheme. This means that the majority of British managers are either appraising their staff, being appraised or both, normally once a year. Our own training experience suggests that the appraisal interview is seen by managers as one of the most difficult and important interviews they have during the year.

WHY ARE APPRAISALS DONE?

Given the enormous amount of time, resources and energy that go into appraisals, what do companies hope to get from these systems? The IPM survey found that the main purposes of performance review schemes were to

- assess training and development needs
- help improve current performance
- review past performance
- assess future potential/promotability
- assist career planning decisions
- set performance objectives
- assess increases or new levels in salary

They also found a shift in emphasis from their last review, from assessing future potential towards improvement in current performance, although somewhat surprisingly the number of companies using such schemes for the assessment of salary increases has hardly changed. This finding was different from findings of recent US surveys. Eichel and Bender found that 90 per cent of companies surveyed saw pay as the main purpose of performance review. This was echoed by the Bureau of National Affairs with 86 per cent, and Lacho, Stearns and Villere with 80 per cent of companies.

Looking at the UK survey, it is clear that organisations use their appraisal schemes to achieve a variety of differing purposes. Again De Vries had a similar finding in the US, with a number of organisations giving the following list:

- administrative decisions, such as salary
- promotion
- retention/discharge
- counselling
- training and development
- human resource planning
- validation of selection techniques

It is hardly surprising, when managers are trying to meet a long list of objectives, with the inevitable emotions associated with assessing and feeding back these judgements, that appraisal interviews loom large in their minds as among the most difficult or important they have to perform.

PROBLEMS TO BE MANAGED

This is not a book on the design of appraisal systems, but systems do raise different issues to be managed. These need to be understood, not to modify existing systems, but because the vast majority of managers have to cope with the consequences of the systems their companies use.

Performance review, salary and performance improvement

A number of companies have schemes which directly link pay to performance. Numerous publications exist, for instance *Staff Appraisal: A First Step to Effective Leadership* by Randell, Packard and Slater, which suggest that the salary review and performance review for improvement should be separated in time (up to six months). The reasoning for this is that if you sit down with your manager to discuss how you could improve your performance, then there is an assumption that there is room for improvement. The discussion might include looking at examples from the last year, where performance could have been improved, or even where you made mistakes. You would need to feel free enough to admit these mistakes, so that together you could think about possible improvements. You would need to be able to learn from your mistakes, not to be punished for them. The problem comes when pay is included in the discussions. Most people would tend to concentrate on their successes during the last year, and be much more defensive about under-performance. This often produces arguments that no better could have been done in the circumstances.

The separation of the salary and performance review discussion is worth considering, but it is not the whole story. Firstly, the need for improvement does not necessarily imply mistakes. True a number of improvements do stem from poor performance, but given the increasing rate of change companies are facing, however well the company performed last year, it is unlikely to be good enough in the future. After all, one of the main planks of Japanese management is constant and continual improvement. The following is a quote from Peters and Waterman on the way successful companies achieve productivity through people:

> The people orientation also has a tough side. The excellent companies are measurement-happy and performance-orientated, but this toughness is borne of mutually high expectations and peer review rather than emanating from table-pounding managers and complicated control systems. The tough side is, in fact, probably tougher than that found in the less excellent and typically more formal systems-driven companies, for nothing is more enticing than the feeling of being needed, which is the magic that produces high expectations. [...] People like to compare themselves to others, [...] and they also like to perform against standards − if the standard is achievable and, especially if it is one they played a role in setting.

What are the implications of this for appraisal interviews? The first point is that these companies generate high expectations of performance and results. High expectations lead to high levels of disappointment, they are the opposite sides of the same coin. Why is this? High expectations will mean stiff, but achievable targets. The stiffer the target the greater the risk of not achieving it and the increasing likelihood of failure. Compare this with international athletes who are constantly setting themselves targets. They do not expect to set new world records every time they race, but if they race badly you can almost see the self-disgust on their faces. When they have run well, even if they do not win, you see the satisfaction they feel and the knowledge or belief they can do better. It is this mixture of a realistic sense of achievement and a dissatisfaction with the current level that drives them on. The same is true with successful companies. Perversely, therefore, they have more 'failures' than average companies. What sets them apart is not only their achievements, but the way they handle failure and disappointment. It is the mixture of recognition of achievements and tolerance of failure that enables people to take risks, innovate and become high achievers.

The other point to come from this quotation is that these companies are measurement-happy and performance-orientated. Good and poor performance are, therefore, highly visible, and the reward systems have to reflect these results or major dissatisfaction would follow. These successful companies, researched by Peters and Waterman, do not seem to have the same problems in linking performance review, improvement and salary.

We think therefore that managers should not simply accept that people will be defensive about their performance, when hard cash is involved. It is possible, even essential, to confront the issue. Even in companies where the culture is not this way inclined, individual managers can still achieve this with their own subordinates and build relationships where high achievement is expected and rewarded, where poor performance is confronted, but when risks are taken, failure can be learnt from and accepted.

We will look at how to handle this in the appraisal interview later, but the first step is an analytical one. Although a manager's job may not change substantially year by year and the same job description may remain valid for some time, it would be very unusual if his six key accountabilities had the same priority ratings year by year. For instance, a production manager in a factory may have been responsible last year for planning the introduction of a new product into manufacture. His priorities this year would be to increase the quality and manufacturing efficiency of that product. Next year it might be to reduce the manufacturing cost or implement a new labour agreement. In all cases his fundamental job would not have changed, but the emphasis would be very different.

In this sense if you or your manager were to review your performance for the last year, implicitly or explicitly, this performance would not be judged solely against a generalised notion of the job. It would also be judged against the priorities that the business or organisational situation established for that job. This does not mean that any development needs identified during this review are invalid, but whether they are things you should concentrate on in the next six or twelve months would be dependent on the job priorities during this period. One does not want to success-fully motivate staff to invest energy and commitment to developing unnecessary or untimely skills and knowledge.

Ideally at the end of an appraisal you want to agree on a balanced view of the strengths and weaknesses and the successes and mis-takes of the subordinate in relation to the job demands over the last year. Similarly the improvements not only need to relate to the past, but also and more importantly, to the perceived job demands of the future. It is for this reason that a separation between reviewing last year and looking forward is a good idea, although this separation usually has to be managed within the same interview.

Performance and potential

A number of appraisal schemes still have the identification of potential as one of their aims. Certainly the companies we worked for at the start of our careers had appraisal schemes which were totally dedicated to longer-term development needs and potential for career development. Now when other aims have been added, like performance improvement within the job, this still remains the major or only source of data on career or skill needs for manpower planning purposes. However, there are a number of potential problems or pitfalls for managers, whose appraisal systems include assessment of potential.

The first problem concerns the kind of outcomes and feedback from potential assessment. Because they are development needs related to jobs in the future, they must be more generalised than assessments relating to something the person is going to concen-trate on in the next few weeks or months. To draw an analogy, for a company to have a target to improve profitability in itself is no use. The real issues are should it sell more, increase its selling prices, reduce its manufacturing price, reduce stock and so on? The same is true of development targets. If they are too general, they are difficult to relate to current activities. To be told that it would be beneficial to develop such and such a skill, but have no opportunity to use it is at best liable to be confusing, at worst demotivating. It is essential that development goals are translated in terms that make sense or connect to the individual's job. Of course, in many compa-nies staff or management development departments would do this, but even if this happens the process should start in the appraisal interview.

The second problem is the relevance of performance in the

current job as an indicator of potential for other jobs. We have all come across, for example, the best salesman, who when promoted makes a poor sales manager. The criteria one would use for judging current performance may be very different from the criteria used for judging promotability. Certain parts of the current job would provide a better indication of potential than others. It is vital for the review of current performance to be separated from the review of potential, or the opportunity exists for the subordinate to concentrate on activities, which are more in the interest of his own development. If these activities do not coincide with current job requirements, you could find yourself criticising your subordinate at the next appraisal for poor prioritising of work, when he is convinced he has been doing what you wanted.

Another problem is managing career expectations. Certainly in many organisations the appraisal interview provides the only formal occasion for manager and subordinate to discuss career issues. Advancement motivates many people and very few turn down the opportunity to be promoted. If the subordinate is ambitious, while he may be defensive about weaker aspects of the year's performance, he will be listening for positive feedback in areas where he performed well. He will then perceive the appraisal as confirmation that his expectations and aspirations are realistic. The danger for the manager in coping with these expectations is that comments like 'Of course, being able to manage a budget is essential if you're going to become regional manager' may be heard as 'When you're able to manage a budget, there's nothing to stop you becoming a regional manager.'

This is an example of the pressures and influences that individuals bring into interviews. It is not the only danger in dealing with potential in appraisals. The manager's own aspirations may influence the interview. People frequently assume most people are like them and, therefore, the temptation to transfer one's own expectations to others is great. Rationally we know individuals differ in their ambition. However, the temptation is there and is particularly strong when under pressure. Emotional appeals are used and promises made, because essentially they are what we would like to hear ourselves.

Be careful not to respond to those pressures this year, only to create a problem later. Use your feedback skills to check that the other person has understood.

The last issue about potential and expectations concerns the trend, which the IPM survey found, to extend the performance review system to include clerical and skilled or semi-skilled operatives. As we have already discussed, the assumptions about potential for managers imply promotion, advancement and career development. However, in our experience, companies who have extended their appraisal systems to include clerical and blue collar workers, usually mean something different by the word potential for this group; it usually means the ability to be flexible. They are using appraisal schemes to support the development of multi-skilled clerks or operators. There is nothing wrong with this, but when the same words and superficially the same systems are used for different purposes, to judge different things at different levels and in different parts of the organisation, the risk of confusion about what the system is trying to achieve is clearly increased.

When designing a form for non-management staff, do not assume that the management form will do. Do you really need the word potential? If you do, be sure that enough time is spent discussing it, so that the meaning of potential is clear and understood. Be careful. Potential is usually synonymous with promotability and can build false expectations, and if it does, will discredit the scheme.

WHO OWNS THE SYSTEM – PERSONNEL OR MANAGEMENT?

Unfortunately, in some organisations the appraisal system is seen to be owned by and operated for the benefit of the Personnel Department. If this is the case in your organisation, then a number of your colleagues are probably going through the motions with appraisal interviewing, rather than seeing it as a process to help them with their job. Some of your subordinates' previous experiences may make them very sceptical about its value, and their commitment to the interview with you may be limited. When you are committed to the system, it is very easy to misinterpret the subordinate's attitude.

Although some paperless appraisal systems now exist, the majority require the manager to complete and use a series of forms produced by the Personnel Departments. These forms can be very useful during the preparation and planning phase see page 135. They will help clarify the purposes of the system; identify the ground that needs to be covered during the interview, identify any agreements that need to be reached and so on. They are not helpful for structuring the interview. The temptation just to complete or talk through the form is considerable, especially if the subordinate has to sign it, as some systems require.

If the form is used in this way, the structure of every appraisal you do, will be the same, whether it has been a good year or a bad year, whether there is considerable change in the job or there is no change. This cannot be right. The structure needs to be appropriate to what you are trying to achieve.

WHAT MAKES AN APPRAISAL EFFECTIVE?

Purpose

One of the central themes of this book is that effective interviewing is dependent on clarity of purpose. Without an understanding of why the interview is taking place it becomes impossible to judge its effectiveness, or to know when the interview has finished or what information is relevant. Clearly, in the case of appraisals, it is not an easy task to clarify purpose, given the likely list of purposes the organisation will expect its managers to achieve. This is not just a problem of magnitude, but also of kind: some of the purposes relate to the organisation and require the results from many appraisals to be aggregated (career planning and training loads), while others relate to individuals, such as reviewing performance or setting performance objectives. The purposes also relate to different time perspectives. Performance review, for instance, looks at the last one or two years, target-setting from the present to a year hence, while assessing potential may have a five-year timescale. We look at these in more detail later in the chapter, but it is clear that these differing purposes require different information and need to be managed in different ways, and that different relationships need to be established to achieve the desired results.

In Part 1, we distinguished between overall purpose and the initial outcomes to be achieved. A manager is not going to improve a subordinate's performance in an hour-long interview. It will happen over the succeeding days, weeks or even months. When the manager is clear about his overall purposes, he must, therefore, identify how far he wants to go on each purpose during the interview. In the chapter on managing change we discussed the example of getting a subordinate to delegate more to his staff. We noted that this would be dependent on the resistances and driving forces for change, and that it would have to be handled differently for the two subordinates mentioned. Simplifying the discussion, it was adequate to tell one subordinate he would have to learn to delegate to satisfy his ambitions: the other needed constant support and help to delegate, even to the extent of showing him how to do it. In the case of appraisal interviewing it is therefore necessary to take the general purpose, to improve performance, and turn this into a more specific purpose, for instance, to delegate more tasks to his subordinates. This then needs to be translated into an appropriate outcome for the appraisal interview. For example, the purpose 'to delegate more' might be translated into appropriate outcomes such as:

- to recognise that delegation skills are essential for good management, and that he needs to develop them; or
- to develop with the appraisee a way he can delegate control to his subordinates.

If the appraising manager has not thought through the interview in this much detail, it is highly unlikely that his subordinate will understand what he is trying to do, and in this potentially emotional setting the subordinate could become untrusting and guarded. Try answering your boss's question, 'Why do you think last month's results are not so good?', when (a) there are rumours that the Managing Director has threatened that heads will roll, or (b) results have been good this year and this particular month is a mystery.

This is an exaggerated example, but the answers people give are influenced by what they believe is the reason for the question. Clarity of purpose is, therefore, not only important for the manager in appraisals, but the subordinate also needs to understand the purpose.

Balancing criticism and recognition

Because performance review systems are directed towards development or improvement, it is inevitable that a significant proportion of the discussion centres on the aspects of an employee's skills or performance, where changes are thought desirable or necessary. There is nothing wrong with this, but what may feel like a constant stream of criticism needs to be balanced by the recognition of strengths and successes. In fact, one of the most common complaints of managers, with whom we work, is that bosses are quick to comment on under-performance but rarely give recognition for achievements.

We originally found these remarks surprising, but we now find their constancy and repetition depressing. After all, it is over twenty years since Herzberg published his findings on motivation. The name is commonly known by managers, but not the results of his research. We therefore make no apology for briefly including them. After all people should not only leave appraisal interviews with a clear view of improvement or development areas, but should be motivated to do something about them. The following is a quote from Charles Handy:

> Herzberg maintains, on the basis of his research studies, that in any work situation you can distinguish between the factors that dissatisfy and those that satisfy. The interesting thing is that they are not the opposites of each other. Dealing with the dissatisfying factors does not turn them into satisfying or motivating factors. In general, the dissatisfying factors are things to do with conditions of work – company policy and administration, supervision, salary, interpersonal relations and physical working conditions. He called these the hygiene factors. They are the necessary conditions of successful motivation. The satisfiers are achievement, recognition, work itself, responsibility and advancement. These he called motivators. Good hygiene deals with the question 'Why work here?', only the motivators deal with 'Why work harder?'

We have been working for the last two years in a jointly owned United States and European telecommunications company. This company has development establishments in the United States, Holland and the United Kingdom, and a number of Europeans have worked in the States and vice versa. In the United Kingdom establishment, where we have been involved in appraisal training, there is an interesting phenomenon. Despite using exactly the same system, job descriptions and criteria, the American managers consistently give higher ratings than their European counterparts. Although we have not accurately researched this, we feel that the difference stems from the American belief that it is always best to encourage people, while the European feels that the correct way is to point out faults and to be accurate. Underlying this are two other assumptions – results are more important, or methods are more important. We have used the names, American and European, as shorthand to label the two differing beliefs. While this is appropriate for the situation in this company, we do not mean to suggest that Europeans are not interested in results or that Americans are unconcerned about methods. However, we do think that individuals and organisations differ in the relative importance that they give to each position. It is important to understand this for appraisal interviewing, not just to ensure consistency between different managers operating the system, but also to aid communication within the interview itself.

These different belief systems not only value different things, but would be critical of each other. For example, the 'methods' manager would say that the 'results' manager would have a tendency to overlook problems or weaknesses, which may be important in the future, even if the short-term results are good. Or the 'results' manager would say that the 'methods' manager would have a tendency to find fault, concentrating on this rather than building on and recognising strengths and achievements, and demotivating his staff in the process.

Imagine an appraisal interview in this telecommunications company, between a stereotypical European manager and an American subordinate, where the manager has not considered that there could be differences of values and belief. The year's performance being reviewed is satisfactory, not brilliant. There are areas where improvements would be beneficial, but there is no real concern since the performance is adequate, if somewhat uninspiring. The tendency of the manager would be to concentrate on the improvements that would be desirable. Given the values of the subordinate, it would be reasonable to assume that he would expect some recognition for the achievements of the last year. The subordinate would feel that, as these had been dealt with rather quickly in the interview and most time had been spent discussing improvements, last year's performance had not been good, and in fact the desirable improvements are essential to achieve a satisfactory performance. In this case this is not the message the manager wanted to communicate and the possibility for further confusion would exist, when the subordinate, for instance, receives an average salary review.

We are not saying that people are simply results-orientated or methods-orientated. People feel that both are important, but individuals and organisations will vary about the degree to which they feel they are important. The key point is that what an individual believes will affect his expectations: what he expects will affect what he hears and what that means to him. Our values and beliefs as managers, therefore, influence our ability to communicate with our subordinates.

ARE RESULTS MORE IMPORTANT TO YOU THAN HOW THE JOB IS DONE?

Think about a piece of work you have done recently, which you were pleased with. Why were you pleased and how would you describe it?

Take an example of a piece of work that one of your subordinates has done, with which you were not wholly satisfied. Why were you not satisfied? What was your subordinate's view of this work, and does it match yours?

Take an example of a piece of work that one of your subordinates was pleased with. Why were they pleased? Were you pleased?

Can you identify anything your subordinates do, which irritates you?

From your answers identify the values which are important to you about work and how it should be done.

Do the same for your subordinates.

Remember it is the differences that hinder communication.

THE QUALITY OF APPRAISALS DEPENDS ON THE QUALITY OF INPUTS

Peters and Waterman in their book *In Search of Excellence* found that successful companies saw their people as the primary source of productivity gains, not capital investment. To achieve these gains, their attitude to their staff was crucial. They treated their people as adults and had respect for the individual:

> That basic belief and assumption (respect for the individual) were omnipresent. But like so much else we have talked about, it's not any one thing – one assumption, belief, statement, goal, value, system or program – that makes the theme come to life. What makes it live at these companies is a plethora of structural devices, systems, styles, and values, all reinforcing one another so that the companies are truly unusual in their ability to achieve extraordinary results through ordinary people.

To us this confirms and reinforces our own experience of appraisal interviews and can be predicted by our model of interviewing. Honesty is vital for success. Nobody would seriously suggest that successful business strategies are based on an unrealistic assessment of the company's present state. There are numerous techniques to help develop this assessment, such as SWOT analysis or the Boston Matrix. Yet the use of a good or appropriate tool will not guarantee success, if the answers it requires are inadequate or false. For instance, to convince oneself that the company's products are 'Rising Stars', when in fact they are 'Cash Cows' or even 'Dogs', may engender short-term feelings of comfort, but will certainly produce long-term or medium-term disaster. The same is true of appraisals: to ignore or not provide the deserved recognition to a subordinate will lead to dissatisfaction, and the best staff will probably leave to go to jobs or companies where they do receive it. Conversely, to avoid confronting a problem, to save embarrassment or awkwardness, is liable to perpetuate the problem. The link with Peters and Waterman is that it is difficult to see how one can respect the individual, if one is not honest with them. Research on self-appraisal systems has shown that individuals tend to be more critical of their own performance than their managers are. The question is not, therefore, should I be honest in appraisal interviews, but how should I be honest?

The other similarity with the Peters and Waterman quote is that they stress the theme of respect pervading all the organisation's systems and structures. Appraisals provide the opportunity to review performance over, say, a year, to identify trends or emphases, but they can only be as good as the information available for this period. In this way appraisals are dependent on the quality of the work reviews and the feedback during the whole year. We have met managers, who save up points to make to their subordinates in appraisals. This is not necessarily deliberate, but given the pressure of 'what can I say', the manager has, in his mind, gone back over the year and identified some point which was not discussed at the time. They are then surprised when the subordinate gets angry, saying in effect, 'If it was that important, why did you not say anything about it at the time?' Or the individual may feel if the manager can only raise issues that were not important enough to mention at the time, he is 'nit-picking', and the whole appraisal process is trivialised.

The appraisal interview, although different in purpose from the manager's other activities, is dependent on them. The expectations both parties have, will not only be determined by their views of appraisals, but also on how they have worked together in the past. In this way not only is the subordinate's performance under scrutiny, but implicitly how the manager has managed is being reviewed.

These are a number of factors that influence the design, implementation and running of appraisal systems. Managers who are given a system to operate need to understand some of the design issues, as they will have to cope with and manage the consequences. For example, if the performance review for pay occurs in June, and the review for improvement in December, it may help the manager deal with the subordinate's defensiveness when discussing improvements. The manager will, however, have to ensure that the relationship between the two events and between rewards, pay, and performance are understood, otherwise unrealistic expectations may be generated. Of course, this assumes there is a connection between rewards, pay and performance, although not necessarily a direct one. It would, however, be a strange organisation, if no connection at all existed. On the other hand, if the system the manager is operating does not separate in time the performance review for pay and development, the connections may be clearer, but the manager will have a harder job ensuring the subordinate is not too defensive to discuss improvement. The way to handle the differing purposes and issues is through the structure of the appraisal interview.

The Appraisal Interview

Having discussed the key issues to be managed in appraisals, we will use our 'model of interviewing' to consider the interview itself.

PURPOSE AND DESIRED OUTCOME

We have discussed the importance of this earlier in the chapter and do not wish to repeat it here, except to point out that before you can determine how to manage the interview you must of course be clear about what you are trying to achieve.

Try to determine your outcomes, taking account of the following:

- What motivates your subordinates? Will this help you or create resistance to change?
- How do your subordinates learn and change?
- How will you have to reinforce and support any improvements and developments?

You will need to ensure

- that the improvement and development targets and tasks relate to job priorities;
- that the timescales of the targets and goals relate to the timescales within the job;
- that any activities that come from the appraisal will be followed up and monitored.

HOW MUCH CAN BE PLANNED IN ADVANCE?

In Part 1 we identified a number of factors that determined the ability to plan interviews. To remind you, they were:

- Is the outcome known?
- Are there procedures to follow?

- Do you know the relevant facts that will be discussed? Are
  you clear about the content of the interview?
- Can you control the content and structure of the interview?

As we have been stressing, a number of the outcomes need to be
clear, and will be. However, this will not necessarily be true about
all the outcomes. There are two areas where the outcomes could be
unclear.

The first area which may be unclear is how far you will get in
discussing a particular topic. An example will clarify the point. You
are appraising a salesman, who gets good results, but you have had
a number of comments about his abrasive manner, from some of
your key customers and you feel you cannot ignore it any longer. In
dealing with this issue there are a number of stages that must be
covered:

1. Get him to accept there is a problem.
2. Explore and identify what he does that makes people feel
   he is abrasive.
3. Develop ideas to overcome the problem.
4. Develop skills and new ways of working.
5. Monitor the feedback to check the problem is overcome.

Not all of these stages could be finished in one interview, but it may
be possible to achieve the first three. The key point is that each
stage is dependent on the previous stage being successfully completed. For instance, there is no point in trying to identify the
behaviours which make him seem abrasive, until he has understood
there is a problem and accepted that he must do something about it.
In this sense the stages can be thought of as a hierarchy of outcomes. As a manager you can be certain of the minimum you need
to achieve, but you can only decide during the interview whether
you can continue or will have to pick up the issue at another time. In
this particular case the salesman may be aware of his problem and
may have spent a considerable time thinking of ways of overcoming
it. If so, in the appraisal you could help him decide what to do about
it. On the other hand he may have been unaware of the problem.
You might then decide that he needs time to think and to accept the
feedback you are giving him.

The idea of a hierarchy of outcomes gives you a structure for
dealing with an issue. It not only identifies the sequence of events,
but it also identifies the points where decisions and agreements have
to be made. Remember, it is not only the appraiser who takes the

decision to continue. It is essentially a joint decision. After all it is unlikely to be effective, if the reasons for a problem existing are being explored by the appraiser, when the appraisee has not even accepted that there is a problem.

The second area where uncertainty occurs, is when the person being appraised has some outcomes of his own that he wants to achieve. These may coincide with the manager's outcomes, be in addition to the manager's outcomes, or be in conflict with the manager's outcomes.

It may be possible for the manager to predict what the subordinate would hope to achieve during the interview, but there will always be surprises. What the manager can predict with a high degree of certainty is that the subordinate will have his own desired outcomes. Therefore the manager must plan that there is time during the interview for them to be raised.

Earlier in the chapter we discussed the relationship between appraisal systems and the personnel function. In most appraisal systems there are procedures that must be followed or information that has to be given. Where this is the case, the manager can and should plan these sections of the interview. The manager will often, in these parts of the interview, be using his presenting skills, and this gives him control over the information that is presented and its sequence. This is particularly helpful when the appraisal system requires the manager to communicate a topic or information that could be emotive, such as a performance rating.

The manager's ability to plan will vary in different parts of the interview. For example, when the manager is reviewing the subordinate's performance, it is vital that he has the relevant facts. Part of the preparation the manager needs to do is to identify illustrative examples from the review period, which will reinforce and clarify the points he is making. This again implies a sequence in presenting the information, namely presenting the idea, then giving an example to illustrate. If you reverse this sequence, notice the effect. It will feel to the subordinate that you are generalising from a specific case. If you can avoid this, you should. After all, you do not want your subordinate to produce another example, which to him proves the opposite. You are not trying to create a debate between politicians: trading examples is rarely helpful in management. It emphasises differences, when you are trying to promote agreements. It will also hide your message, since it is only the argument or disagreement that is remembered.

The manager will, therefore, have a clear understanding and knowledge of the content of the appraisal, when he is reviewing past performance. This enables him to control the structure of the interview, although he must leave ample opportunity for the subordinate to express his views.

When the appraisal moves on to look at future activities, the situation changes. The manager will still have control over the structure of the interview, but the content may be less familiar. The manager will be encouraging the subordinate to produce ideas, some of which will be new to the manager. He will, therefore, be unable to plan in detail this part of the interview. However, he can direct the interview to its outcomes, by ensuring that the structure is clear, both to himself and the appraisee. This will enable him to use his feedback and summarising skills to manage the appraisal.

THE RIGHT ROLE FOR APPRAISALS

From what we have said earlier, it will be clear that when performance is being reviewed the manager will be in an executive role. The subordinate will have expectations that he will be told what his boss thinks of his performance. We do not mean to imply that this requires a monologue from the manager. A discussion would be more appropriate. But at the finish, it is essential that the subordinate understands the manager's view.

When dealing with improvement and development needs, the situation is much more complex. It will be appropriate to be in an executive role when identifying an improvement need, but choice exists when the appraisal moves on to how those needs can be met. In the chapter entitled Managing Change, we identified the key resistances and motivations that people have to changes and the appropriate roles that are necessary to deal with them. The choice of role should, therefore, be dependent on the ideas mentioned in that chapter. Remember the role you choose should not be based on which role you feel most comfortable in, but on its appropriateness to the change issues of the subordinate.

The consequence of this is that the manager will be changing roles several times during the interview. It is for this reason that appraisals are one of the most complex interviews that managers undertake. The effectiveness of the appraisal will also be dependent on how successful the manager is in changing roles.

CHANGING ROLES IN THE INTERVIEWS

We probably all know someone who is very good at telling you what to do — who occasionally asks you what you think as though he is consulting you, but then by his actions demonstrates that he is not interested. When we change roles, however, our behaviour has to change and be consistent with the new role.

The following extract shows how role is changed successfully in an appraisal interview. A Personnel Manager is reviewing a new training course with her subordinate the Training Officer. The course has recently run for the first time and has received critical reports. The Personnel Manager does not want this situation to occur again and has spent the first part of the interview discovering what happened. We are joining the interview at the end of this discussion.

------▶
AN APPRAISAL INTERVIEW

Personnel Manager: OK so I think we're agreed. The problems with the last course were that the managers were not fully aware of the course objectives and its content. So some of them sent unsuitable participants. Also the major case study was too simple and a new case is required for the course. You will be contacting the Administration Manager to arrange that.
Training Officer: Yes, I think that's fair.
Personnel Manager: Well let's move on. I know later in the year you're planning to run the updated Supervisors course. Given what we have just talked about, what's the best way for us to introduce that course into the company?
Training Officer: I think we need to involve the managers in developing some of the cases and perhaps get some of them to lecture.
Personnel Manager: How do you think we can involve them?

So what has the Personnel Manager done?

1. Summarised the main reasons for the critical reports.
2. Checked that this is agreed.
3. Indicated that the topic has been dealt with and that she wants the interview to move on.
4. Introduced a new subject.
5. Asked an open question as the first attempt to establish a consultative role.
6. Followed this with another open question, built around the key word 'involve'.

7. Used language that reinforces the consultation: 'What's the
   best way for *us* ...' Not you.

To ensure a consultative role was established, the Personnel
Manager would have to continue to ask open questions. She
could also use closed questions, not to gain information, but to
check that she had understood the information she had eli-
cited.

$$\longrightarrow$$

PRESSURES AND INFLUENCES BROUGHT INTO APPRAISALS

Appraisal interviews, like other interviews do not exist in isolation.
They take place within an established relationship. Past experiences
are bound to influence what people expect to happen. If the subordinate has found appraisals to be productive in the past, then he is
likely to enter the interview expecting to get some benefit from the
discussion. He may also expect the process to be hard work and
challenging, with both parties having the opportunity to voice their
opinions. If, on the other hand, his experience has been that
managers go through the motions to satisfy the system, then he is
likely to be uncommitted to the interview, even if he is committed
to the ideals of the system. The manager will have to constantly
probe and question to demonstrate that it matters to him. Accepting
his comments at face value will run the risk of confirming his
expectations. Remember the world of human behaviour is full of
self-fulfilling prophecies. People look for information that confirms
their views, not the information that proves them wrong.

In Part 1 we identified a number of pressures and influences that
could affect interviews. The following are likely to be important in
appraisal interviewing:

The appraisee's belief about job competence

Most people like to perform their job well. Therefore, this is going
to be a significant pressure, when their performance is being
reviewed. If your subordinate is confident in his ability, he may find
even mild criticism difficult to accept, wanting to concentrate on his
achievements. Conversely, the subordinate who is less confident
may be listening for the criticism which confirms his impression, and
he will be less receptive to praise. If the appraising manager can
predict this, it will help him to choose an appropriate balance of
stressing problems and recognition.

The appraisee's career needs

In Part 1 we discussed how career needs may make it hard for subordinates to be open with their boss. However, the ambitious subordinate may interpret all the comments the manager makes in terms of promotability. If this pressure is not understand and recognised, then the purpose can shift to answering the question 'When am I going to be promoted?'

The organisation's culture

This will often feel like a pressure, both for the manager and the subordinate. It will make certain roles more legitimate or acceptable than others. For instance in 'informal' cultures there may be a tendency to adopt an advisory role, when an executive role may be more suitable. In other cultures managers are paid to take decisions and decisiveness is valued. Therefore, to consult can be seen as indecision and to be avoided.

The demands of the manager's job

Managers are usually busy, work long hours and often feel they are pushed for time. The temptation to 'tell' subordinates rather than to advise, educate or counsel is great. Certainly in the short term it can save time, but the manager is likely to have to return to the same issue again. In this way more time invested during the appraisal will be economical in the long run. However, if this is impossible, the manager must modify his outcomes and recognise that he will have to find time later.

A more detailed discussion on values, expectations and pressures will be found in Part 1. The importance of identifying the pressures is that awareness helps you to manage them in the interview. The consequences of poorly understood and mismanaged pressures can be:

- the purpose is lost.
- differences in values and expectations can lead to miscommunication.
- de-skilling of both the manager and the appraisee.

SETTING THE RIGHT ATMOSPHERE FOR THE INTERVIEW

You know your own staff and the type of situations in which they feel comfortable. However, the following are points to consider, which will help you to establish the appropriate emotional climate for the appraisal.

Explain how you are going to manage the appraisal

Your subordinate will have things he wants to discuss. Structuring his expectations, so that he can decide, for example, when it is sensible to raise points, will help both of you control the interview. Also telling him that there is time for his views, will start to demonstrate that you believe what he thinks is important.

State early in the interview how the year has gone

One of the expectations subordinates will have entering an appraisal is that the boss will tell them what he thinks of their performance. Even when they are sure of what the boss thinks, they will still expect it to be confirmed. The longer the interview continues without the manager giving his opinion, the more likely it is that the subordinate's uncertainty will grow. Managing uncertainty is never easy. It is always easier to manage certainty, even if that certainty creates disappointment or anger. This process of bringing views into the open works both ways. Take the example of poor performance, when the manager is unsure how the subordinate will react. The boss may hint and imply that problems exist, to test for reactions. The trouble with this approach is that if there is no reaction, it becomes increasingly difficult for the manager to come clean. The inevitable result is that when the subordinate finally understands, he may or may not be annoyed at the news, but he will certainly be annoyed at the way he was 'told'.

Be open if you want the subordinate to be open

The research on body language has found that in successful communication, the body language of participants matches each other. The same is true at the emotional level in interviews. You cannot expect the subordinate to trust you, if you do not respect his point of view. You cannot expect him to disclose his doubts and worries, if you are not prepared to express your opinion.

Try to meet some of the subordinate's desired outcomes

This of course may not be possible, if these outcomes are in conflict with yours. In most situations, however, this will not be the case. If the subordinate's needs are forgotten in the process of a manager achieving his objectives, then the subordinate will feel the manager is unprepared to collaborate and attempts to consult will become very difficult. You can also expect the subordinate to feel disappointed. The more important the subordinate's outcomes are to him, the greater will be the disappointment.

SHOULD I ASK THEM HOW THE YEAR WENT?

A common piece of advice in books on appraisals is that the manager should ask the subordinate, how he feels the year has gone. Certainly this provides the manager with information, which he can use to feed back his own view of the year. But consider the following exchange, which takes place after the explanation of why they are meeting.

Manager: Well now, we are agreed on the purpose of these appraisal interviews. I wonder could we start by you saying how you think the year has gone?

Subordinate: Well, I think it was quite a good year really in the circumstances. I'm certainly quite pleased.

Manager: What do you mean in the circumstances?

Subordinate: Given that it has been a very busy year, and on top of that we had the launch of the new range of toiletries, which have gone well.

Manager: Yes, I agree the new range has gone well, but the launch was delayed.

Subordinate: That was because we couldn't get the advertising space we needed.

Manager: And why was that?

Subordinate: Well when we came to book the ads we discovered that our launch coincided with another couple of major projects and the space had already gone.

Manager: How long up front did you try and book the ads?

Subordinate: The usual time.

Manager: Do you think that was sensible, given how many ads you had to co-ordinate to get the impact we wanted?

Subordinate: In retrospect, no.

It is clear early in this exchange that the manager's view of the year's performance is not the same as the subordinate's. The subordinate is starting to justify himself and very soon he realises that his boss does not hold his 'rosy' view of the year, in other words he

gave the wrong answer to the question 'How do you think the year
has gone?' The manager is communicating what he thinks, but it is
not stated. It is implied by the questions. Therefore, it is liable to
generate responses such as, 'What's the point in telling him when
he's not listening?' or the subordinate may become defensive or
suspicious, or an argument may even develop.

None of these are feelings or reactions that the manager would
want to create, if he is trying to establish a relationship where the
subordinate feels able to trust him and talk openly about his performance and his needs.

If it is not always appropriate to ask the question, how can you
tell when to use it and when not? The rule is simple. As the manager
you have to be confident that the subordinate's answer broadly
matches your own view.

The question will work if you both agree it has been a good year.
It will work if you are pleased, but he is not so sure. It will even
work if you both think the year's performance is not so good, but it
will always be inappropriate if the subordinate's view of his performance is greater or better than your opinion.

But why is the question appropriate in some situations and not
others? The answer lies in the kind of emotional climate you are
trying to build. To be able to reassure your subordinate that his
perception matches yours will help build confidence, and this in turn
will promote openness and trust. Also when you are trying to reach
agreements about future action at the end of the interview, it is
always helpful to start with an agreement.

Conversely, if you are unable to reassure and agree, a statement
of your point of view would be more appropriate. Although this
may give you the subordinate's disappointment to manage in the
interview, you will have been open, honest and will have committed
yourself. This may not immediately elicit a reciprocal response, but
is is unrealistic to expect a subordinate to behave in this manner, if
the manager is demonstrably not being open and honest. Trust is
earned, not imposed.

STRUCTURING THE INTERVIEW

One of the central messages of this book is that the manager must
be clear about the long-term purpose of the interview and what
specifics he is trying to achieve in a particular meeting. In an
appraisal interview this is complex. We have already mentioned
that from the organisation's point of view most appraisal schemes
have a variety of differing purposes. Overlaid on this, are the

particulars of the individuals and their performances. The generalised organisational purposes must be translated into outcomes, which are appropriate for the individual. Some of these outcomes may be achievable in one interview, such as telling them their performance ratings. Others, such as developing a knowledge and skill in an additional application of computing, will only be achieved in the following months. In this case, the desired outcome from the appraisal interview may be to accept that this is a need or to plan how to develop these skills.

Given this diversity of purpose and outcome, it would be surprising if a single structure was appropriate for all possibilities. Imagine yourself having two subordinates in the same role, one having performed well and who you would see developing into a broader role, the other whose performance is unsatisfactory. You may be required by the appraisal system to review last year's performance and to set improvement and development targets for both subordinates. However, the balance between improvement and development, the relationship that needs to be established and the involvement of the subordinate in identifying development needs, would differ in both cases. Nevertheless, some general points about structure can be made.

Statement of purpose

We can think of no situation where it would be inappropriate to state the purpose of the interview at the start of an appraisal. In fact, we think it is vital that you do state it. As we mentioned earlier in the chapter, the reasons people feel are behind the questions they are being asked influence their answers, and if their perception of why you are asking questions differs from your reasons, then the answers will not be the kind of answers you want. For instance, they may be defensive or non-committal, when you are trying to stimulate openness.

In fact, we would go further than this and say that it is desirable for the purpose to be understood prior to the interview, so that the subordinate can prepare for the meeting. Then restate it at the beginning of the appraisal, together with a statement of how you are going to conduct the meeting. The subordinate will almost certainly have points to make or questions to ask. It will help you to manage the interview, if the questions get asked at appropriate times. The appraisee will certainly feel happier if, when the interview has finished, he has raised all the points he wanted to.

Structuring the expectations of the appraisee on why he is there and how the meeting will be conducted can only be helpful to you both.

Producing the interview structure

In the section 'How much can be planned in advance?' earlier in this chapter, we introduced the idea of a 'hierarchy of outcomes'. In the example of the abrasive salesman the following series of outcomes for an appraisal interview were identified:

1. Get him to accept there is a problem.
2. Explore and identify what he does that makes people feel he is abrasive.
3. Develop ideas to overcome the problem.

To continue the analysis, while it is not possible to be specific about what roles would be appropriate without knowing the individual, it is likely that the manager would have to change roles during this sequence. For example for the first outcome an executive role would be appropriate; when the salesman has accepted there is a problem the manager could counsel or consult with him to identify the reasons; finally the manager might advise on possible courses of action.

In this way three 'mini-interviews' with the salesman are identified. Each has an outcome, a beginning and an end, and an appropriate relationship that needs to be established. In some situations, it may be best to have the simplest structure and to create three distinct interviews. For instance, where the salesman may be resistant or previously unaware of the problem, leaving time to think may be desirable. However, in most appraisals it will be possible to achieve more than a minimum outcome. The importance of recognising these mini-interviews is that it not only identifies the key parts to manage, including role changes, but gives you a sequence to follow.

This does not mean that each mini-interview in the sequence immediately follows each other. There is another factor to consider, the time perspective. All appraisals systems are part of the process of ensuring better use of human resources in the future. Even where the major emphasis is on reviewing the previous year's performance, this is still true; for the process of reviewing and rewarding should certainly reinforce desirable behaviour and highlight or clarify what are undesirable actions or incomplete knowledge and skills. This is based on the belief that what happened in the past is a reasonable indicator of what should and can happen in the future.

For instance, the majority of managers would expect good performance to positively influence their rewards or promotion possibilities. Given this expectation, it makes no sense in an appraisal to discuss the future before the past has been reviewed or before its connection to the future has been understood. In fact, without this an appraisee will probably interpret a future development need as a deficiency in his performance and skills, even when it relates to new responsibilities and tasks.

In structural terms, therefore, the appraisal interview has to accommodate the sequence of mini-interviews that derives from the hierarchy of outcomes and the past/future separation. This gives three basic structures:

1. *Time-determined structure.* Review the past performance completely, then discuss improvement and development needs.
2. *Issue-determined structure.* An aspect or responsibility of the job is reviewed and then improvement or development targets are generated. This is followed by reviewing another responsibility.
3. *A combined structure.* A number of areas of responsibility are reviewed. A common issue or theme is identified and this is used to consider improvement or development needs. This is then repeated with another group of responsibilities.

In each case the mini interviews provide the detail to the structure, including decision points and role changes.

How you decide on the appropriate structure

The answer lies in the state of mind, in which you want the appraisee to leave the interview. In all appraisals the manager wants the subordinate to leave the interview believing that he is capable of improving his performance or developing his skills. But this is not all. The subordinate should ideally be motivated to achieve these goals. Certainly the appraisal will not have been successful if the subordinate, even after reflection, is less motivated than when he entered the interview.

Let us consider an appraisal of a subordinate whose performance has not been good. If the issue-determined structure was used, what would be the result? The manager would raise an issue of poor performance in an area of the job, then follow up to produce ideas to overcome the problem. Having reached an agreement or acceptance, he would then raise another problem. In other words, as the subordinate starts to feel things could improve, he is presented with another problem. In the end he would feel like the boxer who keeps getting up off the canvas only to be knocked down again. In this situation it would be better to use the time-determined structure, review all the performance, then identify the improvement targets. This builds towards a positive ending, finishing with an emphasis on what the subordinate can do to improve.

In the case of appraising good performance, the other structures are more appropriate. By considering an issue or theme and following this through, the manager will reinforce the achievements by emphasising a sense of progression and development. For the high performer, this is liable to be highly motivating, for not only would he be receiving recognition for his performance, but also for his continuing development.

The structure is, therefore, determined by choosing the option which enables the manager to end the interview in the most positive way, given the circumstances. If 'bad news' has to be given in the appraisal the manager should not lead up to it, explaining as he goes and finishing 'Therefore ...' He needs to get the issue into the open, so that the remaining time can be spent on the more productive activity of what the subordinate can do to resolve it.

It is the last few words and the feelings a person has at the end of an interview, that stay in their mind. Structuring and planning the appraisal is the way of ensuring that the manager has control and the ability to determine what those words and feelings are for the appraisee.

-->

CHAPTER ELEVEN

The Counselling Manager

Have you ever needed help from your boss? Have you had some bosses who are easy to talk to, and some who do not seem to have the time, or are not very interested in your difficulties? Are there some subjects which you have found easy to talk about, and some which you could never talk to the boss about? Are there some difficulties which you would find impossible to discuss with anyone at work? Are there some problems that you would be able to talk to a friend about, off the record, but would not be able to ask for help with in a more formal situation?

You would not be unusual if there were some circumstances where you were able to ask for help at work, and others where you were not. Using the model of interviewing, the values you hold will mean that there are some things which you will discuss at work, and others which will be kept in your private life. These are often things which you might like to discuss with your boss, but because he has some influence over other parts of your life, like your career, you define them as private. Sometimes there are subjects which are easy to discuss with the boss, for example a technical difficulty you are having with the job, but you might find this a little more difficult if several people have recently been made redundant, and they were not technically competent. You may have discussed personal problems with your boss before, and it is clear that he is uncomfortable talking about those kinds of things. If you are a woman, you may have noticed that your boss finds it difficult to talk to you about certain things. You may also have learned that your boss has very different views or values from you, so that you feel he will be unhelpful or unsympathetic.

-->

SITUATIONS WHEN IT COULD BE DIFFICULT TO ASK FOR HELP

The Case of the Missing Report

You have been working almost full-time for the last two

weeks on a report for senior management on a new system which will improve order-handling substantially. You are excited about it because it is a good system and will show a very fast return. The meeting which will discuss the report is in two days time. Last night you were working late at the office trying to get as much completed as possible without any interruptions. The boss is very particular about things being done to time, and has had a word with you a couple of times about your reports being late. You were well pleased with your work and confident that you could put the finishing touches to it today.

When you tried to get the report up on your personal computer this morning, it was clear that you must have erased it last night. You were uncertain about the commands when you had to switch everything off last night. You have requested training on the computer several times, but the time is never right. There is a lot of pressure in the department to work directly onto the computer, especially when there are spread-sheets and graphics involved as there are in this report.

The problem now is what to do about the report. You still have all the data and your rough notes and will be able to do another report, but it is unlikely that you will be able to complete it before the meeting. In any case, the chairman would normally have a copy today, and that is out of the question.

You will have to talk to your boss quickly. He will attend the meeting, and will have to ask for a delay and explain what has happened. He may be able to ask for the meeting to be rescheduled.

How will you approach him? Will you feel able to be completely honest about what has happened? Or will you find an excuse that puts you in a less bad light? Will you find it easy to search with him for a reasonable solution to the problem?

The Case of the Missing Orders

You have been working for your present company as a sales representative for four years. During that time there have been changes in sales managers, changes in territory, and changes in products. Most recently, the territories have been changed again, and you have lost a number of key customers, whom you have been working with for all the time you have been with the company. Since these changes have been made, the monthly sales returns have shown that your figures are not meeting target. The boss has asked to see you.

How will you approach the interview with him? Will you feel that you want to protest about how unreasonable the changes have been? Will you want to present your case for getting some of your old customers back? Will you try to get the sales targets adjusted?

The Case for Advancement

You have been talking to your wife recently and she has been pushing you to see your boss about promotion. She says that the mortgage has gone up again, apart from the other expenses, and she is finding it difficult to cope on your money. You have been in your present job for over four years, so in some ways you have a reasonable case. On the other hand, most of the younger people who have been recruited in the last couple of years have been better qualified than you.

You do not really want to start studying again, but your wife has said, and it makes a lot of sense, that the only way you are going to get on is to get the same qualifications as them. You have decided to see the boss and tell him that you want to start evening classes, or even better you would like the company to give you day release to undertake your study.

Will you tell your boss that this is mostly your wife's idea? Will you tell him that you are finding it hard to manage on the money? Will you tell him that you do not really fancy starting your studies again? Or will you present your case in a rather more positive way?

The Case of a Father's Shame

You are 39 years old, and have tried to live your life by good moral standards, as your Christian beliefs are important to you and your family – or so you thought until last night. You have two children, a 17-year-old daughter and a 15-year-old son. The boy has always been a very active lad, good at sports, popular with his friends, and often in minor trouble with his teachers for his noisiness and 'over-enthusiasm'. Your daughter, on the other hand, is quiet and rather studious. She is good at music and likes to be on her own, and you have tried to encourage her to go out with friends. In fact, you have been delighted that recently she has been going out more with some friends from school.

Last night the police came to your house to tell you that she had been arrested with a number of other girls for shoplifting. They wanted to search your house for stolen property. They said that they had been watching the girls for several weeks, as it was clear that they think this is an organised gang. Your daughter is being held in custody, because they say she is the ring-leader.

There is nothing you can do today, and your wife has advised you to go to work so that you can keep occupied. She has said that she will call you if there are any developments.

Your boss has just met you in the corridor, saying that there are a number of errors in some paperwork that you completed this morning, and he noticed that you were not looking yourself at lunchtime. He has asked you to go to his office in half an hour and have a chat. He is not someone whom you like particularly. You do not have much in common, but he is quite a good boss.

What will you be able to say to him? You would probably feel that you would like as few people as possible to know about your daughter. Especially at this stage, when it might all turn out to be a big mistake. Will you try and keep the conversation on the mistakes you made this morning, and say you are not feeling well – after all, this is true! What if he finds out later? He will think that you have misled him. He is a decent enough man, and will probably understand. Anyway, you would want to keep the conversation as brief as possible, in case your wife rings with some news.

$$\longrightarrow$$

In all these cases you would have good reasons for not telling the truth or at least not the whole truth. It might well be that the boss would be able to help. Indeed he might want to help. In that sense he might want to be the counsellor, but you would have good reasons for not letting him do any counselling.

In The Case of the Missing Report you might well want him to be executive, and reschedule the meeting without discussing what has happened at all. In the Case of the Missing Orders you would probably like him to listen to reason, your reason, and then take action. In the Case For Advancement you would not want him to probe for your real reasons, but simply to agree to the study leave. In the Case of the Father's Shame, you would probably prefer that the interview did not take place at all.

These examples highlight the major difference between counselling in the traditional sense of marriage guidance, or in social work settings, and counselling for the manager. The subordinate and the manager have to cope with the other relationships they have, which could influence pay, career or performance.

Many managers would be happy to help their subordinates solve their problems, but if you recognise the difficulties in the cases above, you will see why helping cannot be a simple, rational, problem-solving process. The subordinate may deny that there is a problem, they may cloak it in different terms, or present it in a way which they feel would be acceptable to their boss. They may simply want the boss to confirm the answer which they have already thought of, and not want to explore any options. All of these things can make it very difficult for the manager to help, even when he has the time, skill and inclination to try.

WHEN DO YOU FIND IT HARD TO ASK FOR HELP?

Answer the following questions. They will help you understand the difficulties that you face in being completely honest with your boss.

What are the problems that you find it easy to talk to your boss about?

> Technical difficulties?
> Lack of knowledge about the organisation?
> Getting work completed on time?
> Difficulties with the budget?
> Finding it difficult to work with colleagues?
> Not being able to control a subordinate?
> Future or career issues?
> Problems at home?
> Personal or medical problems?
> Any other problems?

What are the problems that you find, or would find difficult to discuss with your boss?

Can you identify the reasons?

Has this changed with different bosses? If so, in what ways?

Are there some things which you would usually try to conceal from your boss?

Are there others which you would sometimes conceal?

What are the factors which are likely to make you conceal them?

Are there some things which you can honestly say you would never try to conceal from your boss?

How do you think your subordinates would answer these questions. It will give you an insight into the areas, in which they may find it hard to accept help from you.

WHY IS IT DIFFICULT FOR SOME PEOPLE TO ACCEPT HELP?

Sometimes it is difficult to admit to ourselves, let alone other people, that we have difficulties. It can be clear to everyone else that a person is not coping with their job, but they may not be able to see it for themselves, much less ask for help.

We may be afraid of what the other person will think of us, especially if it is the boss. It is not unusual for bosses to say 'Why didn't you come and see me before?' But if the subordinate's fear is 'What will the boss think of me if I cannot cope?', he will continue to pretend there is no problem.

We may not be sure we can trust the other person. Your subordinates will not find it easy to admit any work difficulties they have, when they are unsure if the judgements you make will affect their appraisals, or the kind of work you allocate to them. This is not usually a conscious thought-process, but at certain times they may even be concerned about how the discussion could affect their career. It is possible for the lack of trust to be based on fantasy. We have known people on courses who are not prepared to admit that there is anything that they can learn, because they are convinced that we will be passing reports to their company, even when we have made it clear that this is something we would never do.

We may fear becoming dependent on someone. Many people are very independent, especially about their personal lives, and believe that they should be able to solve problems for themselves.

We may be looking for someone to agree with us, or sympathise, rather than resolve any difficulty. When an employee goes to see the personnel officer to complain about the way the supervisor is treating them, and the suggestion is made that a meeting is arranged with the supervisor to iron out the difficulties, it is not unusual for them to say that the problems are 'not worth making all that fuss about'.

We may feel that our problems are unique. We often feel that no one else can really understand, because our situation is different, or even if someone else has had similar problems they were not complicated by so many other factors. It may, therefore, feel that it is not worth discussing it with anyone.

We may feel that our problem is too trivial to seek help, especially if the other person is the boss. It can be very difficult for other people to come and talk to the boss, when they view you as a much more senior person. In their eyes you may be concerned with major strategic issues, meeting important customers, attending important meetings, and, therefore, would not have the time or the interest to concern yourself with their small problem.

Counselling is a way of working with other people, which takes the problems of helping and being helped into account. In the jargon of counselling, it is 'client-centred', that is helping the other person to solve their own problems, to develop their own skills or knowledge. Counselling demands that the 'client' takes responsibility for their own difficulties, that they decide what actions they can take, and in the process learn to take greater responsibility and make decisions for themselves. This is a very useful skill for managers to acquire, but it is essential to try to understand the position from the other person's point of view.

If we take the cases at the beginning of the chapter, we can analyse them in terms of what help would be useful to the subordinate, and what difficulties they are likely to have in asking for help.

Help for the Case of the Missing Report

Initially the subordinate is likely to be having strong feelings of panic. There may be disbelief that the report has been erased. There may be confusion about the importance of this item to the meeting, and there will be a strong concern about what the senior managers will think, and indeed what the boss will think about his foolishness in losing the report. None of these things may be clearly in his mind, they are quite likely to be jumbled up, but what he will almost certainly need is the opportunity to express these feelings of panic.

Once this has been done, he will need help in sorting out the real issues which have to be dealt with and deciding what actions he should take. He may be saying something like 'What's the point of preparing a report now? The opportunity to present it will have passed, and I shall look such a fool that it will have no credibility anyway.' He will need to know that there is some point, that the item can be scheduled for the next meeting, and he will need to be helped to plan a realistic time-scale for producing a new report. He will also need some assistance in thinking through what will be said to the chairman, and to decide if he should do it, or if it would be helpful for the boss to do it for him. At some point he will need some training in operating the computer, but this is probably something which is best left for another time.

As the manager you will not know any of these things until he starts to talk to you, and the pressure will be on you not to panic or be angry since the meeting is in a couple of days. These are feelings you will have to contain, if you want to help your subordinate to deal with the problem.

This interview could start like this:

'An awful thing has happened. I'm very sorry, but it's not my fault. I know this report was being rushed too much, and I have asked you to give me some training on the computer several times. I don't know what we can do now, with the meeting so close. I think we will have to ask for the report to be considered at the next meeting. I don't know how long it will take me to do all that work again ...'

It will probably be very unclear what he is saying, and your initial purpose may be to help him clarify that, and then to decide what your next purpose will have to be.

Help for the Case of the Missing Orders

What help will the salesman want? For you these changes may be important and welcome, but for him they are just one more change. Indeed, one for him which does not make sense, since his best customers have been taken away. He needs to find a reasonable explanation as to why that should be. He will probably feel threatened, because he will know that he has not been meeting his targets and he will need sufficient time to tell the boss why things are going wrong. He will need help to overcome this defensiveness and then he can be helped to think of alternative ways of reaching his sales targets, and to plan the courses of action which will bring that about. There is usually nobody more demotivated than an experienced salesman who is not meeting his targets, so any help to do that will be welcome in the end. It will not be easy for him though, because to get that help, he will in a sense have to admit to himself that he is 'failing', and that will need a lot of help and support.

This interview could well start:

'I'm glad that you could find time to see me this morning. I don't understand why the current reorganisation has been done, and it really is very unfair on me. I don't know if you realise, but it has meant that the two key customers, whom I have worked with for many years, have been taken away from me. I can see no reason for this, and of course, having built up my relationship with them over the years, it will now be very difficult to maintain the business at the previous level.'

There are already two purposes on the table as far as he is concerned: to seek an explanation, and to tell you why this decision is not a sensible one. At the appropriate point you can respond to the first one, but you will probably be better ignoring the second, or helping him to see why it does make sense.

Help in the Case for Advancement

At the simplest level he wants to be supported in his studies, and would like that practical support from the company. Would that really be helpful? He would then find himself embarking on a course of study, which he is not sure he wants. He needs help to consider the implications of this, and to sort out the value of the qualifications for his future career. He may also need help thinking out how he will explain all this to his wife, as this course of action will not help financially in the short term.

This is the help that he needs, but of course he may not be able to ask for it from his boss, or perhaps from anyone, but there are likely to be cues in the things he says which indicate the various difficulties which he has.

This interview might start like this:

'Thank you for arranging this discussion. As you know, I've been with the company some time now, and I've been in my current job for over four years, I've been thinking about my future, and it seems to me that if I want to get on, and I do, then I must think about trying to get some appropriate qualifications. I would like to talk to you about the company supporting me in my studies ...'

His apparent purpose is made explicit in this last sentence, but you will need to listen carefully for the cues as to the other concerns that he has in relation to this purpose.

Help in the Case of a Father's Shame

In some ways this could be a very difficult case, because the father may not want any help at all. He would like the problem to go away, and if he does want help it would not be from work. The only help he might feel he needs is for his boss to be understanding and to recognise that the errors will be temporary. Practically this is difficult, because he would have to give some explanation for his absent-mindedness.

Underneath this there are a web of problems, which he has probably not articulated for himself. He needs help coming to terms with the fact that this has happened. He needs to cope with the sense of failure, he needs to cope with the feelings of not knowing his own children, and the worries about what else he does not know. He needs to cope with the shame of having the police call and search his home, and the fact that the neighbours will probably know. Above all, he cannot discuss this with his boss or anyone else at work without having a 'reasonable' explanation. Another problem may be how to carry on at work without telling anyone what has happened. Most of these problems may not even have surfaced for him at the moment, and in response to the shock he may simply be denying what has happened.

This interview might well start:
'Come in Ken, and sit down. As I said to you in the corridor I wanted to talk to you about a couple of mistakes, especially as they are so unusual as far as you are concerned. Then when I saw you in the restaurant, I thought you really didn't look very well ...'
'Oh I'm OK really, just not feeling quite up to the mark today. I'm sorry about the errors. I will get them corrected immediately. What were they? Do you have the papers with you? I hope they have not caused any problems.'
His purpose is to make light of the 'not feeling well', and to keep your attention on the mistakes. Very often when someone moves very quickly from the subject, it is a significant clue, if only in the sense that it is something they want to avoid. In this case you will probably have to wait, but it would be worth another question or two to confirm, or not, your feelings that it is important.

SHOULD THE MANAGER BE A COUNSELLOR?

As we mentioned earlier the word 'counsellor' is often associated with approaches like marriage guidance and social work. In reality, it is a process which all managers should be able to use.

Counselling is the process of enabling people to change. The change may be slight, like helping someone to understand, or it may be a major change in the way someone thinks or feels. The aim of counselling is to assist someone to take more control of their own life, especially during the process of change. The American Psychological Association's Division of Counselling Psychology defines counselling as 'helping individuals towards overcoming obstacles to their personal growth, wherever these may be encountered, and towards the optimal development of their personal resources'. Anne Jones, a leading British counsellor, defines counselling as 'an enabling process, designed to help an individual come to terms with his or her life as it is and ultimately to grow to greater maturity through learning to take responsibility and to make decisions for him or herself' (from *Counselling and Helping* by Stephen Murgatroyd).

If we replace the phrase 'personal growth' with 'growth at work' in the first definition, and 'come to terms with life' with something like 'come to terms with work and its changes', these would be useful definitions for 'counselling in management'. Managers are often told that their staff are their most valuable resource. Counselling is a tool which can be used to help staff both to increase and realise their potential in their current and future jobs. An approach which helps people learn to take greater responsibility and make decisions for themselves will always be a very useful skill for the manager to possess.

In our first chapter we pointed out that partly because managers are paid to make decisions and are expected to be the experts and to provide answers, helping others to value their own expertise, and to make their own decisions, does not come easily. We find that managers can often accept the logic that this process is necessary, indeed accept that there is a better chance that people will be committed to decisions that they have made themselves, but they are quickly seduced into the role of expert or decision-maker.

Sometimes it is not possible to be the expert, for instance, when a specialist works for you, who possesses a much higher level of technical knowledge. Similarly it is inappropriate to be the expert in personal and domestic problems, where there may be differences of values and expectations. Even if you have never been in a counselling position with someone with a domestic problem, you have probably had a colleague or friend talk to you about a personal problem. Do you sometimes think, as they are telling you about it, 'I don't know why you see that as a problem'? Or as you start to explain the obvious logical answer, do you find that you are making no sense to them. They point out all the reasons why you do not understand.

This is often recognisable by what we call the 'yes but syndrome', where all your helpful suggestions are met with 'yes but', and then the reasons given why they will not work. It is often a subtle and polite process, but it feels as though they are ungrateful, and that they do not want your help. This may be true, but it is more likely that you are offering 'expert help', when what they need is help to solve the problem for themselves – counselling.

Counselling is like being an interested sounding-board. We have probably all had someone come to talk to us about a problem and we have just sat quietly and listened, nodding occasionally, and maybe asking the odd question to help our understanding. The person may talk for some time, and then leave saying how helpful we have been. As they go out the door you probably think, 'I'm glad it was helpful to them, but I really didn't do anything.' Sometimes that is all counselling means – sitting and listening. The other person may have thought everything through for themselves, and they need to check that it makes sense. They trust that you will spot the weak links in their thinking and will ask the questions that will ensure that they cover everything they need to.

In organisations, managers often use uninvolved colleagues in this way – particularly those who will sit and listen rather than offer yet another idea which frequently confuses or complicates the issue. If you are one of life's natural 'problem-solvers', you are quite likely to get involved with the issues, be interested in the other person's thinking and solutions, and be searching for an improvement. You are then in an 'expert' role and not acting as a counsellor, helping them to resolve the issue for themselves.

The key to successful counselling lies in the way we asked you to think at the beginning of this chapter. Try always to identify what help the other person needs. Usually you will need to listen first. Let them tell you in their words, and do not assume that you know what the problem or issue is *from their point of view*. Careful listening will enable you to identify their need for help in what we have called the Thinking Cycle, or the Action Cycle. For example, in the Case of the Father's Shame, he is not yet clear what problem he wants help with, if indeed he wants help at all. He is still right at the beginning of the Thinking Cycle. In the Case of the Missing Orders the salesman has been round the Thinking Cycle, deciding on the problem, generating some solutions, and evaluating their effectiveness. He has already moved into the Action Cycle, planning out the steps he wants you to take to improve things. If you are to be effective with him you will have to take him back to reformulating the problem, so that he can see for himself that those action steps are not appropriate.

If the nature of the help someone needs is just planning the action steps, they will find it very frustrating if you take them back to rethinking the problem, and often this would be quite inappropriate. However, if their thinking has been based on a wrong, or unhelpful definition of the problem, this may be exactly what is necessary. For example, it is not unusual for people to see their difficulty as someone else's fault, and the solution, therefore, is to change the other person's behaviour. 'I know I am often late, but the trains never run on time. The company should put pressure on the railways to improve their time-keeping.' A reformulation of the problem in terms of the employee not getting up early enough will lead to rather different solutions, and ones that the employee has some control over.

Thinking and action cycles in counselling

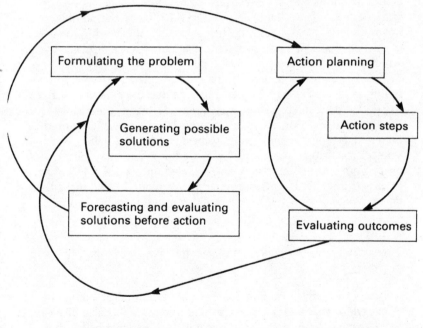

The process of counselling in work is usually

1. Identifying where the other person is in their thinking
2. Testing the appropriateness of that position in the cycles

3. Helping the other person move through the stages of resolving their problem, and especially to move from the Thinking Cycle to the Action Cycle.

This last point is very important, or the counselling process can become a way of talking about things and never getting round to taking any action. It may be therapeutic to go round the Thinking Cycle many times, and in grief you will often hear a person talk about the death of a loved one many times over. In management this can only go on for so long, before the subordinate, or other person is moved into the Action Cycle with a question like 'So what are you going to do about it?'

Ideally the person being helped will go through all of these phases, often not as tidily as this diagram suggests, and will be encouraged to do all the thinking for themselves. The manager acting as counsellor should listen, reflect back what has been said and question what is said. This will help to clarify the points which have been made. Summarising the points, or paraphrasing them will often help to define the problem. It also helps to separate issues which are jumbled together in the person's mind. Sometimes it will be necessary for the 'counsellor' to suggest other ways the problem might be seen, or suggest other solutions that the person is not able to see for themselves. They may even advise the other person to take particular action steps, if learning from experience would be unhelpful to the person or the business. Be careful. When you find yourself advising, suggesting or prescribing you may be moving away from counselling, and being seduced into the problem-solver, or expert role. Let the other person do the work. Indeed make them do the work of thinking for themselves if you possibly can.

------▶

WHY IS IT SOMETIMES DIFFICULT TO GIVE HELP OR COUNSEL?

Apart from the fact that we are better trained at being the expert, so that this is a more familiar role to us, it is also nice to be seen as the expert. It can make us feel important or useful.

If we define 'boss' as someone who ought to be able to provide the answers, we may feel pressured to be the expert when logically this is not possible. If it is their learning problem, their divorce, or their career, it is quite likely that they will see the issues differently to you.

If the other person is defensive or sees things differently, the temptation to argue or persuade can be strong. We all know managers who enjoy a good argument, and whilst this can be very productive in some circumstances, it can be very unhelpful when the situation demands listening, and trying to understand the other person's point of view.

We tend to deny other people's feelings, because we would not feel the same in their situation. It is not very helpful for the accountant to say to the manager, who is uncomfortable with figures, that there is nothing to worry about. Telling the redundant employee who is terrified about what will happen to his family, that he has been made redundant but should not worry as his family will cope perfectly well, may make him feel even worse.

We may confuse counselling with being soft. Some people assume that counselling means over-praising rather than creating a supportive situation where faults, weaknesses, or difficulties can be challenged and discussed. We recently had a man on a course, who had major difficulties in dealing with senior people. It would have been accurate to tell him that he had very good skills, and could sort out what he wanted to do, so that this difficulty should not be a problem. It would have been of no help. We needed to create an atmosphere, where he could describe the feelings of difficulty *as he saw them*, recognise the nature of the problem that he had, and evaluate the steps that he could take to overcome this.

Sometimes we change the subject without explanation, because we are thinking differently about the problem. If we are not trying to think with the other person, and to understand how they are working on the problem, we will see connections which will not be obvious to them. This can be very confusing. The connections need to be made explicit. Sometimes you will want to refer back to something they said some time ago, and link it to something that has just been said, and this needs to be made clear. 'You said a few minutes ago that you do not want to continue with your studies, and you are now saying that you would like to pursue promotion. How do you reconcile those thoughts?'

Similarly, people will change the subject when they feel uncomfortable. We often find, even in the training situation, that a 'counsellor' will ask a question which brings the problem almost to the surface, and then as it begins to emerge they will change the subject and move to safer ground. This can be conscious, and will be rationalised with the explanation that they thought it would be too difficult for the other person to explore it. Or it may be quite unconscious. In either case it is likely to be the feelings of the counsellor which are being protected. In general, people will only talk to you about something that they are willing to explore, and they can always regulate how far that exploration goes. Creating a feeling of trust, and then denying someone the opportunity to talk, by changing the subject can be very frustrating.

We may see a possible solution and present it to the other person, without recognising that they are not ready to accept it. In redundancy counselling it may be important in the earlier stages of transition for the person to deny that their redundancy had anything to do with their personal skills or abilities. They may need to go on believing that they are competent, whilst they deal with all the fears about loss of status, identity, and their concerns about the family. Once some of these fears have been allayed, it may be possible for them to confront the fact that their skills are to some extent outmoded. To confront them with this when they need to go on blaming the company could be quite destructive.

$\longrightarrow$

These are factors which may make it difficult to counsel. We certainly find that some people are 'natural counsellors', and find listening and working from where the other person is both easy and satisfying. Other people are the natural solution-providers, and they have to work very hard to restrain themselves.

At the same time counselling in a work context is rarely the same as traditional counselling such as marriage guidance. In that context you would only counsel someone who is willing to be counselled, and the role is one of facilitator, helping someone come to their own satisfactory decisions about their marriage. The manager may be trying to do something similar, but he is also the representative of the company and this can add another dimension.

A successful counselling interview which has manifestly helped the interviewee is exhilarating for both parties. But the interviewer may have to be careful not to commit himself, or the organisation, to action beyond his authority or ability to carry out. Since the counselling manager will have company responsibilities due to his position, he will probably need to change at some stage from listening to persuading or inferring. He may need to say 'I have heard and understand your point of view, now listen to mine.' He may need to reiterate the company policy, restate departmental policy or standards, or call attention to the person's poor past record.

The timing of switching roles, in terms of our model, from counsellor to advisor or executive is critical. If it happens too early, or because the manager is feeling uncomfortable, the counselling may be over before the problem is identified, or before the person is able to do anything about it.

Sometimes the person being counselled will try to push the counsellor into an inappropriate role. The subordinate may push the boss into taking a decision, and then the boss carries the responsibility. The colleague may ask 'What would you do?', demanding expert advice. That way they do not have to think about the issues or make a decision. If the solution does not work, it is the adviser's fault. We do not mean to imply that this is a conscious process but it certainly happens, and it is a trap for the manager who is not a 'natural counsellor'.

The appraisal interview is difficult because it will frequently have these changes of role. The manager will need to be executive for parts of the interview, for example presenting his review of the last year, but in other parts he may need to be the counsellor, for example helping the appraisee to formulate a plan of action to improve performance for the next year. It is so easy for the subordinate to say, 'Well, what do you think I should do?' and if the manager is not careful, he starts to advise or prescribe, and has lost his counselling role. At each stage the skilled manager will be deciding if the most appropriate task is for the subordinate to think things through and decide for himself. If this is so, then the manager must stay in the counselling role, using the Thinking and Action Cycles we discussed earlier, to decide on the help that the subordinate needs to resolve his problems.

You will also need to think about any reasons why the other person would find it difficult to be helped. These may be the values that they hold about you as a person, or about bosses, or they could be the influences that they bring into an interview which you try to set up for counselling. You will need to be aware that these kinds of factors may be creating difficulties. Often it means that counselling will take time. You will have to do something to reassure the person that you can be trusted, or that you really do have an interest in their problem. You may need to say something about yourself, and that you have got into a similar problem, not to provide the answer for them, but to demonstrate that you do not think any less of them for having the problem. We talked with a bank manager recently who told us that with some customers he had to wait over half hour before they were relaxed enough to talk to him about the problem, which they had made an appointment to discuss. Sometimes as a manager you may have to give people time to relax if the issue is important to them.

We talked in Chapter 3 about the extent to which an interview can be planned, and the amount of control which the interviewer can have. For some interviews, or more likely for some part of the counselling interview, the other person will need to be in control, but it does not mean that the manager has lost control of the whole interview. In the redundancy interview the manager needs control of the early part of the first interview, so that the task of telling the person that they are being made redundant is completed. Once the person begins to react, and certainly in subsequent counselling interviews, the subordinate will need to be given much more control, so that they can raise the things that they want to discuss, talk about their fears and concerns, and have the opportunity to ask questions. This suggests that in managerial counselling parts of the interview will be planable, while other parts will be controlled by the interviewee, with the manager being unclear in advance of the subject matter. What is certain is that if the manager is unwilling to relinquish control, preventing the interviewee from talking about the problems in his terms, effective counselling will not take place.

When counselling simply means 'helping' then it could be appropriate to tell someone what they should do, or to advise them of the best action for them. In this way the immediate problem may be alleviated. Some people want this kind of help, and some subordinates think that this is an appropriate relationship to have with the boss. Often it will be necessary to give the subordinate more control of the discussion, so that they are pushed to think and make decisions for themselves. This may be part of the learning they need to do to develop their potential for problem-solving and decision-making. In the short term they may not thank you.

If the manager wants to encourage more self-sufficiency, less dependency, more willingness of people to take their own decisions, and probably more commitment to those decisions, he will need to do more things in the top half of this list. That means more control will be given to the subordinate. Of course, there will be times within the interview, when the manager may need to advise, suggest, and even prescribe, but if it is really a counselling interview the balance of behaviours will need to be those from the top half of the list.

We have found that for many managers the key problem in counselling is not the lack of skill, but convincing themselves that it

Control and counselling

Increasing Manager Control	Counselling Behaviours	Increasing Subordinate Control
↓	Listening Drawing out Reflecting Clarifying Questioning Summarising Suggesting Advising Prescribing	↑

is all right to give the other person control. This means developing an attitude of understanding it from the other person's point of view, and helping them solve the problem, with their own values and pressures, and with their own skills and abilities.

THE THREE BASIC ELEMENTS OF COUNSELLING

The research on counselling has shown that there are three fundamental elements which are important in the relationship of client and counsellor. We think they are important for successful relationships in many situations, but perhaps particularly important to the counselling manager.

The first of these is **respect**. This is behaving in a way which conveys that the other person is worth listening to, unique, and valuable, perhaps even making them feel important. There are some very practical things which you can do, which will convey the feelings of respect, such as,

- giving them your time,
- remembering their name,
- remember the basic courtesies like offering a chair, or a cup of coffee,
- asking questions to show you are interested,
- not interrupting, or talking across what they are saying,
- checking out assumptions you have made about them or about what they have said.

The second thing is **genuineness**. This means conveying that you are trustworthy, spontaneous, and not hiding behind your role. It means

- not pretending to be something or someone you are not,
- responding naturally,
- being spontaneous,
- not being defensive or arguing,
- sharing feelings appropriately.

Perhaps most important is the third element of demonstrating **empathy**. This means demonstrating that you understand the other person's problems, and how they are seeing things. This, by the way, does not imply that you condone it, simply that you understand. It means

- reflecting back to the other person the feelings that you have picked up, with phrases like 'That must have worried you', or 'So you were feeling very uncertain.'
- Appropriately sharing similar experiences.

Many of these skills, or ways of behaving, are the same as or similar to the skills we discussed in Chapter 7. We talked there about managing the emotional climate, and in counselling it is necessary to manage a particular emotional climate, so that the other person feels respect, genuineness and empathy.

Managers often feel that this is all very well for the professional counsellor, but that it is not appropriate for the manager to 'take things too far'. It is better to hand over the difficult problems to the professional. This may mean simply asking personnel to deal with it, or arranging an appointment with an appropriate outside agency. Of course, if you talk to a personnel officer they will often say that the manager is too willing to hand over any problem that looks as though it might be difficult! As usual, the truth is probably somewhere between those two extremes, and there are probably some managers who get too interested in problems and carry on trying to help, when it is way beyond their competence or their role.

It is difficult to define precisely, but in general managers only have a legitimate right to be involved with a problem which is affecting work directly, and then only as far as the subordinate, or person being counselled, sanctions that involvement. Of course, that sanction can be given too freely. We worked with one company where the supervisors seemed to spend nearly half their time listening to the staff's personal problems. This can be a good way of avoiding work, and boss and subordinate can collude with each other to do this. Sometimes the boss can be just plain inquisitive! Try to be honest with yourself that the problem is legitimately affecting work, unless the subordinate has asked for your help. Then try to decide if you are the appropriate person to be helping, and if spending time on it is legitimate work for you.

In organisations the real difficulty is trying to decide when it is sensible to hand the person on to the professional for help. Just because you feel uncomfortable with personal problems is not grounds in itself for asking the personnel department to take over. You may well appear as though you are cold and uninterested. You will have to do enough listening, perhaps helping the person to formulate the problem, discussing with them how they will talk to personnel, and what help they expect to get. In this way you will be able to demonstrate the basic elements of counselling, providing them with a good base for going to see the professional, and maintaining support for them in their own department.

A CASE FOR COUNSELLING?

You were promoted to Regional Investigations Manager three months ago, responsible for South-East England, having moved to London from the Midlands. Reviewing your credit investigators, you realise that several of them will need to improve their performance, but none of them give you problems in comparison with your secretary, Kathleen Reed. You can never be quite sure if she will be at work. She is regularly late for work and quite often takes a whole day off with 'a serious headache'. You tried to be friendly and make a joke of it at first, but twice recently you had to have a serious talk with her. Last time you told her you would have to give her a formal warning if she did not improve. You have never had to issue a formal warning before, and it would be very unusual in the office if you did.

Actually you are unsure what the procedure would be, and when you talked to your boss, he said that it was not normal, and you ought to be able to do something about it yourself without getting Personnel involved.

Kathleen is good at her job, and indeed has been very helpful in settling you into your job. It would be difficult for you if she left, since she knows the administration aspect of the job better than you, and is well liked by the investigators and other members of staff.

However, something has to be done about the situation. Hardly a week goes by without her being late, arriving outside the flexitime bands. When you spoke to her two weeks ago, she said that the buses had been re-routed creating problems, and that she had been having bad headaches which leave her exhausted and unable to come to work the next day. She was half an hour late again at the beginning of this week, and the Divisional Manager had been trying to get a message to you to postpone a meeting that morning. You turned up and felt a real fool. She then took the day out on Thursday. You had a day full of appointments, which was constantly disturbed by the phone, apart from which you could not find half the papers you needed.

You have decided to see her, and must decide what the purpose of the interview will be, and how best to conduct it.

What will your purpose be? It would probably be simplest if you just got her into your office and gave her a formal warning, but you are under some pressure from your boss not to do that or to involve personnel. Let us assume that you decide, in spite of what you said last time, to counsel her before you go into the formal disciplinary situation. What will be the initial outcome that you would like to achieve?

1. To ensure that she knows this is not satisfactory?
2. To find out the cause of her lateness and absence?
3. To help her find a solution to whatever the problems are, so that the situation does not recur?
4. To ensure that she leaves the interview knowing that something must be done or the disciplinary procedure will have to be used?
5. Assuming that she knows there is a problem, to offer her the opportunity of deciding what she can do about it?

This last one is probably closest to the definition of counselling – taking responsibility and making the decisions for herself. If this is not achieved, it does not prevent you as the manager from switching roles to the executive, and making it quite clear that this behaviour cannot be tolerated. However, she probably knows that already, and may well be feeling very guilty. If you start the interview from that point, you may not set a very helpful emotional climate for her.

Perhaps the biggest trap in all counselling interviews of this type is to go for the objective of finding out the causes of the problem. There is often a fascination in the problem itself. This may be helpful, and indeed it may well be what happens in the early part of the interview, but be careful. You may be setting yourself up as the expert. Once you know what the problems are, you may be tempted to become the expert and try to solve them. You may find yourself wallowing in problems that you have not got a clue how to solve, so do not give yourself that burden. Your job as Kathleen's counsellor is to help *her* to cope with her problems in as far as they affect her work. She already knows what those problems are, and she only needs to tell you about them in as far as it helps her to resolve the difficulties, and start arriving at work regularly and on time. Of course, it is often true that counselling will involve the other person telling you 'all about their difficulty' but it is not necessary for the process. You have to be careful not to get so interested in the problem, that you forget what you are trying to do.

In a sense, Kathleen is an involuntary subject of counselling. She would probably prefer you not to say anything – but you have to. It is probably best to assume that she does recognise the problem that her behaviour is creating in work. Verbalise that for her, but do not rub it in, because she will probably be feeling guilty anyway. Then make it clear what the purpose of the interview is – that you want to help her decide what she can do to improve the situation.

The first thing in counselling is usually the recognition and exploration of why the person is not happy about the current situation: formulating the problem. In this case Kathleen may agree that it is not satisfactory, either assuring you that she will try to improve things, or saying that she is very happy at work, but telling you about the headaches and buses again. Remember that what is needed is respect – take an interest in what she says, do not make judgements. Try to understand why she is saying whatever she says. Try to empathise – put yourself in her shoes and try to see the difficulties from her point of view.

Encourage her to move on to saying how she would like things to be. In order to do this she may need to give you further explanation of the problems, but you will need to encourage her to be realistic. If she makes vague promises of improvement, ask her how much improvement she can realistically achieve.

The next step could be to specify the options that she has for making changes. This will often test out the reality of the improvements. If there are vague ideas about the headaches getting better, but she is not prepared to consider the option of seeing a doctor, you may need to question what she really wants to do. If you offer her help with transport, and she is not prepared to try it, you know that this is probably not the problem. You need to help her generate some realistic options, and this may mean suggesting some that she has not considered. For example, you might ask her if she has tried to find anyone who lives near her and could give her a lift. Try to offer the options rather than impose them.

She will now need to select the option or options that she thinks are most likely to help her cope with the problem. Get her to say why she thinks they will help, and in what ways. In rejecting some of these options she may go round the Thinking Cycle several times, and in the process redefine the problem. If you are listening carefully, this redefinition, or even the introduction of another, and perhaps more significant problem will usually be there for you to pick up. If you feel you have been round the Cycle enough times, and you are confident that you understand the problem and she has decided on a possible solution, move her into the Action Cycle.

Supposing you had been through this process with Kathleen and decided that the headaches were only a symptom, and the buses were only an excuse, but there was a very real problem at home which she was unwilling to talk to you about. However, she felt that in the short term it would be alleviated if she could have some time off work. In the longer term she would need some professional support from someone, but she was not sure from whom. The action steps in this case could be to get her to specify how much time she needed, and when she would take it off. Perhaps you could ask what arrangements she could make to cover her own work, and you could also set up an appointment with personnel to obtain the help she needs in deciding which would be the best organisation to talk to.

Here the manager has got Kathleen started on a series of actions, and he would need to provide a bridge forward so that she feels she can tell him how she is getting on, and if she needs any further help. It is important that she does not feel he has 'washed his hands of her'. Having done all that work the manager is probably in a good position to switch to the executive role to specify a timescale by which the improvements in time-keeping must start. It would need to be realistic if she is to believe in the manager's genuineness, but without this the manager is not carrying out his proper role as the boss.

We have in this chapter demonstrated that counselling is a process, and not a type of interview. For the manager it is a process which can be used in many circumstances, where it is most advantageous if the other person works out 'the answer' for themselves. This is usually appropriate when it will be a learning process for them –

something that they have to work out to fit their own circumstances, or where it is particularly important that they feel committed to the outcome. We have demonstrated that this will be so in the obvious 'counselling' interviews, but it will also be useful in many other types of interview. It can be used in work review, in pre-disciplinary interviews, in problem-solving discussions, and often as part of the appraisal.

Counselling skills are some of the most useful tools that the manager can have. They can be used in a wide range of situations, but the counselling process takes thought, practice and patience. In the long run the skills will help to manage people more effectively, providing the manager with more time, because his staff are less dependent and probably more motivated to solve their own problems and difficulties.

CHAPTER TWELVE

Reviewing Work

So far in this book we have concentrated on the more 'special' or 'unusual' interviews which managers perform. While these frequently loom large in the minds of managers as difficult or important interviews, they occupy, in fact, a relatively small proportion of managerial time. In this chapter we are going to look at the more common managerial interviews to do with planning and reviewing work.

We start by reviewing the way managers see the managerial role. Three transcripts of actual interviews are then presented, each with a commentary and remarks made by the interviewer and interviewee.

Managers and Managing

The traditional management theories would see the manager as someone who gets work done through and by other people. To do this he would plan, organise, direct and control. However, the research that has been performed on what managers actually do, paints a different picture. The research of Rosemary Stewart in the United Kingdom found that managers spend up to a third or a half of their time on external or lateral relationships. That is about the same time that is spent on subordinates. Mintzberg in the United States had a similar finding. He also found that managers preferred to be active rather than conceptual or abstract. Tasks that are perceived as non-active, like answering mail, were seen as onerous. In fact, more attention was given to current information, even if its source was gossip, hearsay or speculation. Not surprisingly, they preferred spoken communication, such as telephoning and scheduled or informal meetings, to other forms of communication. Planning was seen to be important, although the researchers found that little time was spent on it.

The picture that emerges is not the one which could be expected from the management theory – the manager as rational man planning, organising and controlling his situation: but rather a person who reacts and responds to stimuli in his situation and directs accordingly. This is consistent with the idea of 'leading from the front' and is reinforced by the work of David Bradford and Alan Cohen in their book *Managing for Excellence*.

They were trying to identify what managers felt was 'a good leader'. This ideal held by managers, even if they failed to achieve it themselves, would still influence their behaviour. They came up with the following points:

1. The good manager knows at all times what is going on in the department. Thus if a boss or peer from another department asks 'What's the status of the Williamson project?' the manager is disturbed if he has to respond, 'I dont know, but I'll check it out for you.' Conversely, the manager feels better about himself, if able to rattle off all the facts and figures.

2. The good manager should have more technical expertise than any subordinate. Thus, if a subordinate in a meeting says in response to a superior's suggestion, 'No, we shouldn't do it that way; there's a new process that is better because ...' the manager feels inadequate. (Although the subordinate wouldn't feel nearly so inadequate, if the boss were to give that response to his suggestion).

3. The good manager should be able to solve any problem that comes up (or at least solve it before the subordinate can). Thus if a subordinate asks, 'How are we going to solve the conflict between Parker and Jennings?' the superior feels less competent if forced to respond, 'I really don't know. What do you think?' (If the subordinate then comes up with a good answer, the manager's sense of competence is further threatened).

4. The good manager should be the primary (if not the only) person responsible for how the department is working. Thus, if two subordinates leave a staff meeting complaining to each other that the meeting was boring and didn't deal with important issues, the boss feels worse than the two subordinates.

Bradford and Cohen go on to argue that this heroic style of leadership is no longer valid in the modern organisation. When organisations existed in environments where knowledge and technology changed slowly, managers were able to know more than their subordinates. Tasks were often simpler, jobs narrowly defined, and managers could observe and judge performance easily: they could answer all the questions!

Modern organisations are no longer like this; the environment is complex and constantly changing, the increase in knowledge and the rate of change in skills and technology is enormous. Jobs have become more complex. Yesterday's way of working, if relevant today, will certainly be inappropriate tomorrow. Complex tasks make it virtually impossible for a person to have all the necessary knowledge, increasing the interdependence between staff, if the work is to be successfully completed. Management, therefore, shifts from direction towards co-ordination or even creating the environment where subordinates can collaborate. Control also changes. The manager can no longer guarantee to out-perform his subordinates, so he has to switch his focus of control from method to results.

We found it hard to believe Bradford and Cohen's results at first, not because we doubted that this situation had existed, but were surprised that they had found these beliefs so prevalent in the 1980s. However, when we thought about it, we have known and still know managers who find it hard to accept ideas from subordinates. The subordinate has to float an idea. It is apparently ignored but reappears as the manager's idea a week later. We know managers who cannot say 'I don't know', and who go to great lengths to cover up what, to them, is ignorance. We also know managers who take every opportunity to demonstrate their knowledge and skill, even at the expense of their subordinates.

Clearly the beliefs and values that a manager holds about his role will affect the way he manages. Some of the pressures and influences that are brought into interviews derive from this view of the managerial role.

The manager will also find some roles easier, more natural and more consistent with certain belief systems. For instance, with the 'heroic model' of leadership that Bradford and Cohen found, there will be a tendency to tell and be executive rather than to advise, or to be advisory rather than consultative.

The importance of these points is that when a manager frequently adopts a less appropriate or an inappropriate role in interviews, it can shift or distort the purpose as perceived by the subordinate. For example, when a subordinate wants to consult his manager and consistently gets strong advice instead, it will start to feel as though the manager's sole purpose is to demonstrate his greater knowledge. The subordinate will in the end stop trying to consult his boss. In these circumstances the subordinate will feel as though the real meaning of the meetings is conveyed by the way they are managed, not the content of the meeting.

The following story, from a company we worked for a number of years ago, illustrates this point. The story is about one of the company's factories, which was managed by an autocratic director, who liked to keep his staff on their toes by asking awkward questions. By asking these questions in his regular weekly management meetings, when all his subordinates were present, he clearly hoped that the public embarrassment and ignominy his managers would feel by failing to answer a question concerning their own area would ensure they did their jobs properly: motivation through avoidance of pain.

Every month financial figures were produced for each production department. This tended to be the first time anybody had seen these results; it was a complicated financial system, so it was always a rush to get the figures ready. The director would look through the results and ask the relevant manager questions about these figures. There were frequently anomalies, for the director to pick on. The public demonstration that the production managers did not know what had happened in their departments and could not explain it, was, as you can imagine, not a pleasant experience. To avoid being surprised by these awkward questions, the managers started to predict the results, so that they could demonstrate their competence, by providing satisfactory answers when asked. The director liked this. His managers clearly were getting a grip on their departments. He rewarded them by publicly praising the managers who produced good explanations. If his policy was working, he should keep it up. After all the director did not want his managers to become complacent. So while he was pleased, he kept on asking the questions, although they became progressively more specific, otherwise he could not catch his managers out. Naturally his managers responded by increasing the detail and accuracy of their predictions and so on and so on.

Finally, the factory had two parallel financial systems, the official one produced by the Finance Department and the unofficial one produced by the production departments. The results from both systems were virtually the same, and this was taken as indicative of a high degree of professionalism on the part of the managers and director. Naturally it is impossible to predict accurately, unless there is a high degree of understanding, and understanding is essential for control. Unfortunately, while the quality of predictions increased, the quality of the financial results from a business point of view did not.

This was not because the managers and director were unaware of the factory's problem, but rather that a whole series of routine and day-to-day meetings were felt to emphasise different goals, more by the way they were conducted than by the content of the meetings. The financial results game was a classic example. After all, it was the director, not the consumers, who controlled the managers' salary and their promotion prospects.

What is the moral of this story? It is not simply that by concentrating on the wrong issue or method, the results were not achieved, but rather that the constant reinforcement of certain behaviours through the way the regular meetings were managed, resulted in management becoming routine. People stopped thinking, even though the evidence existed that the overall company results were not improving. The purpose of the meetings became following the routines and this obscured the real purposes.

In any organisation these day-to-day meetings form the working relationships, whose history, expectations and pressures either help or hinder the achievement of outcomes in the more prepared or formal interviews.

So in many ways this book is written back to front. Why have we done this? In our experience managers are more concerned to prepare for the less regular interviews they have to perform. A manager may prepare the information carefully for the more familiar interview but is less likely to think about how to handle the interview itself. This is not meant to imply that familiarity is bad; on the contrary it can help to build confidence and skills. But managers must guard against the tendency, for instance, to review this month's sales figures by the same method and order as last month's, when the key decisions or actions that come from the review may be very different.

We have constantly stressed the importance of clarity of purpose for the successful management of interviews. This is no less important when a manager and supervisor meet every afternoon to plan tomorrow's production, than it is when they meet annually to have an appraisal.

In the next part of the chapter we present three interview transcripts. These transcripts are from actual interviews. Naturally it has been impossible to include the non-verbal gestures or all the encouraging grunts and 'yeses' that intersperse the words. However, the editing has been kept to a minimum to ensure the feeling of the interview is conveyed, although the names and the situations have been altered to maintain anonymity. Each interview has a commentary on the way the interview is being managed. We also talked to the people involved, and their comments on what happened follow each transcript.

These interviews are not presented as examples of how to handle such meetings, but to provide you with the opportunity to analyse them, using the model and ideas we have given you during the book. It is for you to judge whether the interviews were well managed, and how in similar circumstances you would handle them.

INTERVIEW BETWEEN A PERSONNEL MANAGER AND A TRAINING MANAGER

Personnel Manager:
OK then Joe. We've talked about what has been happening over the last month. Shall we go forward and talk about what work you've got on for the next six weeks?
Training Manager:
It feels very heavy, I must say. I've got a selection course next week, which I've got to work on.
PM: You're actually working on it?
TM: Yes, that's right.
PM: How long is that?
TM: Three days.
PM: Three days.
TM: It's going to take up most of next week. We've got the finance consultancy and the consultants who designed the finance course the week after.
PM: When are they actually coming in?
TM: Tuesday and Wednesday and Thursday, because they're going to interview the managers in order to make sure that the design of the finance course is right.
PM: So they're in, while you're actually on the selection course?
TM: No, no. That's the subsequent week.
PM: Ah, that's the subsequent week.

This part of the interview starts with the Personnel Manager stating what he wants to happen next. This is phrased as a question; he is checking to see if it is all right to continue and that the last topics discussed are completely finished. Rather than getting a simple agreement, the Training Manager makes a strong statement of opinion, followed by a fact. The Personnel Manager now has a choice: does he follow the opinion about heavy workload or the facts about the selection course? He chooses the factual approach, asking closed or specific questions.

The Training Manager continues, by introducing another piece of work, the visit of the finance consultants. This information, as with the information about the selection course, is volunteered, not introduced in response to a question. It is starting to appear as though the Training Manager is producing a case to convince the Personnel Manager that his work load is 'very heavy': his original stated opinion.

The Personnel Manager continues with specific questions to check understanding. Notice he uses his feedback skills and the Training Manager's words to demonstrate he is listening, by repeating the 'three days' and 'the subsequent week'. However, he is only feeding back information which is consistent with his approach. There is no indication that he has heard, let alone agreed with the 'heavy' workload view.

TM: I feel I ought to spend some time with them so that they understand our managers' needs and make sure what the managers say is part of the course.
PM: I think that is very important myself. So, they're in on the ...?

This is the first time the Personnel Manager voices his own opinion and supports his subordinate's decision to spend time with the consultants.

TM: That's the 14th, that week.
PM: The 14th. And you say Tuesday, Wednesday, Thursday.
TM: Yes, that's right. That fills in a hell of a lot in the next two weeks.
PM: To what extent do you think you need to be with them all the while?

The Personnel Manager again ignores the emotive 'hell of a lot' and asks the Training Manager to be more specific.

TM: I don't know the answer to that really. I don't know how good they're going to be or what sort of approach they've got. I feel that I should be there on the Tuesday. If they're the sort of people we like and they look as if they're really going to adapt their work to meet our needs, then maybe that will free up some time, but otherwise I may need to keep quite close tabs on what they're doing.
PM: But it's not your intention to be with them all the while?

The Personnel Manager does not receive an answer which is very specific, although in the circumstances, as the Training Manager explains, this may not be possible. He then follows this with a question which appears to be either another attempt to define the involvement more closely or to check his understanding of what has been said. In fact, it comes over as a statement of opinion and it is clear that the Personnel Manager does not think it necessary for the Training Manager to be present all the time. If the Personnel Manager was checking his understanding the following question would be more appropriate: 'From what you've said, it sounds like you don't want to be with the consultants all the time, if possible?'

TM: No. I don't think that would be helpful. But I do think that some time each day I need to review what they've done and find out what they've discovered, then talk to them about how they're going to apply it to the courses.

PM: Have you fixed the timetable up yet?

TM: No, I haven't.

PM: No, you haven't, so you've got to fix the timetable?

TM: Sorry. I've fixed the timetable for them to meet the managers. Yes, I've done that, so that's all scheduled. But I haven't organised with them when I will see them.

PM: Have you got any help from Pauline to take them around from manager to manager?

TM: Well, working on the assumption that I would need to be with them on the first day, so that I could find out what they're doing, I will do that. If I decided that it wasn't necessary to be with them on subsequent days all the time, then there's no problem in Pauline picking them up after each meeting and taking them on to the next manager. It may be that the managers' secretaries will organise that anyway.

PM: I understand. Let's go on and get the whole picture.

It is not clear why the Personnel Manager introduced Pauline into the discussion. From the answer it is obvious that the Training Manager sees no problem and is slightly dismissive of the subject. The Personnel Manager decides not to pursue the topic and to move on.

TM: Well, the thing that's worrying me quite a lot is that next month we've got these two new courses – the Training of Trainers and the Communications course. Now, we've got agreement on what the design will be. We've done the detailed work in terms of programming it, but there's a lot of work to be done in terms of the detail design of the exercises which will make up those courses.

Quite a lot of work, particularly on the Training of Trainers course to construct the manual that will support the course.

While this is stated as a concern, it is still at a general level. Two courses are mentioned. Although the Training Manager indicates what work is still to be done, it is unclear if his worries are about quantity or quality of work, lack of resources or knowledge, and so on. Is the mention of the manual an example or the concern?

PM: And you're doing that one?
TM: Well, yes. That's right. So, I've got to do the preparation work – that's what worries me – over the next three or four weeks.

Worries again, but how much work is there? The Personnel Manager also needs to separate out the work needed for both courses. While the problems, if there are any, remain at a general level, no help can be given.

PM: How far have you got?
TM: Well, about as far as I've said really. The Communications course – I've got the design work done and I know what sort of exercises are going to be used. I've got a good idea where they can come from and so on, but I haven't really gathered them up or thought about details of each session, as it were.
PM: And you're running those on your own or with someone?
TM: No. I've got Maureen coming in from Newcastle to work with me on that, because she's done good work.
PM: On which one?
TM: On the Communications course. But I think that her expectation is that she will come in for the week of the course and for a few days before to be briefed, but I'll do the detailed design work. So it's quite a lot of work. I mean, it's not massive but it's gritty bits of work.
PM: When you say not massive but quite a lot, what does that mean?

This is good skill: the Personnel Manager demonstrates he is listening by building the question out of the Training Manager's words. He also picks up and uses the rather emotive words used to describe the amount of work.

TM: I don't think I know the answer to that. I don't quite know how many hours of work that is, but there's a few. I suppose I probably need something like two or three days of work to complete that, but then I'm going to have to meet with Maureen and talk the whole thing through. Then there will be the administrative work of actually making sure that the exercises are typed up and duplicated and all that sort of stuff, but I haven't got that far in my head.

PM: It's a new course. You've got the participants lined up, have you?

The Personnel Manager now has an idea of the work load in the detail design. While this is not exact, he feels it gives him enough information to introduce a new line of enquiry, with a short statement and a closed question. As this is the second time the Training Manager has mentioned the time he must spend with Maureen prior to the course, the Personnel Manager must remember to raise this later, or he runs the risk of the Training Manager feeling he is not interested.

TM: Yes. That went well and we got lots of takers for it and so we've selected the first twelve. So that's all done.

PM: I mean, given that it's a first course, do you actually want to go and see them, to brief them, or are you leaving that to the managers?

TM: Well, I thought, given all the things — I suppose in an ideal world I would like to go and brief them, but given all the other things that I've got to do, I feel what I ought to do is write a good brief for the managers and let the managers brief their staff. I know that's not necessarily perfect but it does have advantages, because the managers will actually see in detail what we're doing and what's expected and be involved.

PM: How many managers is that?

TM: That's seven, I think.

PM: Even if you write it up, you're still going to have to spend some time with the managers, aren't you?

TM: Well, not much, probably a few hours at most. In some cases a phone call, to check if there are any questions.

After finding out there is no problem with participants, the Personnel Manager explains the reason for raising the point that it is a new course and asks about briefing. The Training Manager's reply starts with a series of emotional appeals: 'given all the things', and 'I suppose in an ideal world'.

The exchange finishes with 'Even if you write it up, you're still going to have to spend some time with the managers, aren't you?' This question challenges the Training Manager's assumption that a written brief will be adequate. In other relationships it would feel that the Training Manager was being instructed to follow up the written brief with direct contact with the managers.

PM: So, it looks like, as it's the first course, we've got two or three days more preparation, plus how long with Maureen on the course?
TM: Well, probably the best part of a day I would think, going over everything in detail.
PM: And possibly the best part of a day as well with the managers. So that's five days work. OK. So what about the Training of Trainers?

The Personnel Manager starts to summarise, remembers Maureen and adds time to brief the managers. Notice it is not a summary of what was discussed, but a summary of the time that is needed by the Training Manager to finish preparing the Communications Course.

They then discuss the Training of Trainers Course in a similar manner, and we will rejoin the interview with the Personnel Manager summarising that discussion.

PM: So, while the course is about the same length and your time in producing this back-up material is about the same, you haven't got the same problems about the extra time you need to spend with Maureen and the briefing. OK. Is there anything else?
TM: Ah well. The thing that's really worrying me, I think, is that I've got all that work to do and, in a way, it's because we've been pretty successful, that it's got to be done now. At the same time, we've just finished the appraisals and you made the commitment to the board that this month we would produce a training analysis based on the last – well, work based on the appraisals.

Despite the fact that the Training Manager says he is presenting his real concern, he still uses the words 'I think', as he is still unsure what reaction he will get from the Personnel Manager. Notice the use of language: 'I've got all that work', 'we've been pretty successful', but 'you made the commitment to the board'.

PM: It's the board meeting which talks about training and development issues. That's about three weeks away.
TM: That's right. That's right slap bang in the middle of the Communications course that week, you see.
PM: I don't know. I think the Communications course is probably next month.
TM: Yes, you're right.
PM: But, basically, you're tied up next week. You're tied up quite a bit of the time the week after with the financial consultants coming.
TM: I've got all this work for these things, which I mean ...

The Training Manager is starting to appeal to the Personnel Manager, because he still has not got the feedback he wants. This is despite the fact that the Personnel Manager has started to list the work load that his subordinate has.

PM: You've got a week's work for the Communications course.

TM: And the best part of that for the Training for Trainers course. And, you know, in the middle of that lot, I have to try and produce an analysis which – it needs to be a good piece of work, doesn't it? I mean, they like to see that ... Well, they're not fools are they? They know ...

This is a series of emotional appeals.

PM: No, no. There's no point. We've pushed like mad for the managers to do the appraisals over the last three years and put a lot of time and effort into training them, so they can do the appraisals properly. We're going to look pretty stupid and it's going to be pretty stupid, if we don't actually use the output from the appraisals for identifying training needs as well as other things like career development and to establish our priorities.

It is not clear what the Personnel Manager is saying 'No, no' to. It would appear he is agreeing to the Training Manager's view that it is impossible to do the analysis, but this is not said and the purpose of the analysis is not stated.

TM: I don't want to put you into the position where the analysis isn't thorough. It wouldn't be good for development either, would it?

Another appeal, nearly a threat.

PM: I mean, what it looks like roughly is all of those things would keep you busy for six weeks, until after the Training for Trainers course is run. That's assuming there's nothing else. I wonder, given we've always followed the policy in the department that we should be available for our customers, I wouldn't want to think that the Training Manager is, in that sense, not available to talk to anyone for six weeks. Now much of your time is normally spent with people coming to talk about training courses, or managers coming to talk about a development problem. I'm not asking you to be accurate, but is it roughly about 20 per cent of your time?

The Personnel Manager does the right thing by ignoring the appeal and summarising, not the Training Manager's views, but the time commitment of his workload. It is also sensible to check any other

commitments, and he introduces his own view that the Training
Manager has to be accessible. Asking the Training Manager for his
opinion on how much of his time is spent being 'available' is fine.
However, if he wants an answer, he should not provide one himself.

TM: Yes, something of that order I would have thought: 20, 25, per
cent. It depends on the sort of week. The problems with the
appraisals at the moment is that it raised the level of questions. I
think there's more people coming here at the moment, because
they've made their commitments or promises to people about
courses, and while it's on their mind they give me a ring and say,
'What sort of courses are there about this? It's on Johnny's appraisal,
you know'.

Having been given the opportunity the Training Manager is unlikely to disagree with the 20 per cent; it supports his case of work
overload. In the circumstances it is not surprising he gives it a small
uplift to 25 per cent. He then clearly links this to the Personnel
Manager's point a few minutes earlier, about Personnel promoting
appraisals and, therefore, having to respond to them.

PM: So, when you say you are worried about this, are you really
saying, 'It's going to be tight but I can do it' or are you saying, 'I
don't think I can do it'?

Here the Personnel Manager is checking out understanding, and
making the Training Manager commit himself, rather than assuming
what he wants.

TM: I don't think I can do it. I think the timescale is too tight.
PM: It's a problem of success really. You've done a very good job,
and in one sense these Training of Trainers courses and the Communication things have come out of things that you've put forward in
the past, and having created the demand you've got to respond to
it. It's nonsensical not to. Well, if you're saying you don't think you
can do it, then we have to find some slack. Yes? Now, where do you
think you can find some slack? Anywhere?

The Personnel Manager accepts there is a problem and reassures the
Training Manager that it exists because of his endeavours, rather
than his failings. He then starts to investigate whether all the work
is necessary.

TM: I suppose, hopefully, I won't be needed all the time with the
consultants, the financial consultants, so there could be a bit of time
in there.
PM: You could free up another day possibly?

TM: Probably.

PM: But we're trying to find nearly a week. So, what you're really asking me to do, is to see if we can delay the training needs from the appraisal?

Finally the Personnel Manager, articulates the question the Training Manager has been wanting to ask.

TM: Well, I can't see anything else that can give. Although we fix it for this time of the year, it doesn't really matter if it's that week or a week later or a fortnight later, I wouldn't have thought.

PM: Well look, if you can't get it ready for this board meeting, when do you think you can do it?

The Training Manager admits this is what he wants and tries to minimise the importance of any delay. This is ignored and the question 'When will it be ready?' is asked.

TM: Well, if it were a month later that would be great, because the courses would be over. I could put some work into it to get the ground work done, and then get a good report prepared for the end of the following month. That would be after the two main courses, wouldn't it?

PM: Well, I suppose the thing that convinces me, is even if you magically found some time to produce your analysis, the board would get it just before they were going to discuss it, which is hardly satisfactory. What I would like to do, is to be able to tell the board, that because of the new courses you are involved in, all of which are supported by them, that it is impossible to produce the appraisal analysis in adequate time for this month's meeting. They will, therefore, get it by whenever, giving them time to study it, even to discuss it with their managers if they want to, prior to the board's discussion, which I think would be helpful. It does, however, require a date from you when you can deliver it, and it must be kept to. So, when can you do it?

The Personnel Manager sees that a rationalisation for the delay is possible, perhaps even helpful. However, the question 'When can you do it?' has not been answered, so it is asked again.

TM: Realistically, what we are saying, is that it can't actually be produced until next month after the Communications and Training for Trainers course. So, if you want them to discuss it with the managers, we're actually talking about the following month before it's discussed in the board. There's certainly no problem in me getting it ready for then.

The question is still not answered, and the Training Manager uses the fact that the Personnel Manager would like the directors to discuss the report with their managers as a further delay to the board meeting.

PM: Thinking about it, that's no good. It would be three or four months after the appraisals have been done, before they are discussed. I think if we don't discuss it this month, which doesn't look possible, we've got to discuss it at next month's board meeting.

The Personnel Manager rejects any further delay and states when it will be discussed.

TM: So, somehow I've got to produce the analysis for the report. How long do the directors need to have the report, prior to the meeting?
PM: Not long, ideally a week.
TM: Oh well. That might be all right, I suppose. What have we got? There's two weeks after the Training of Trainers courses.
PM: It takes the pressures off you to do it all at once. You may well be able to pinch the odd day in there, when you can start the analysis.
TM: Yes, there should be some time in there to start the analysis. Maybe I can get Pauline to do quite a lot of the clerical work, assist in the office and that sort of thing ... So what it means is that I've got to produce the report by the end of the week after the Training of Trainers course.
PM: Is that possible?
TM: Yeah.

An agreement is reached.

PM: Well, what I would like is a pretty accurate timetable of your time and preparation ... so that if anybody quizzes me about the delay, I can come back with some pretty firm figures.
TM: So you want me to ...
PM: After all, the board agreed about the financial consultants and so on, and recognised the need for that. The other two things were agreed, and we agreed the time and so on. But it would be nice to be able to back it up with some figures that actually show this really is not on, and when we can produce it and stick to that.
TM: I'll do that today somehow.
PM: I don't want to pressurize you too much, because it's important those two new courses go well. The time you said for development and to finish the thing feels realistically tight but achievable.
TM: Yes, it is.

PM: All right?
TM: Yeah. OK then.

The Personnel Manager quickly moves to close the meeting after the agreement is reached. He moves on to think about how to sell his agreement to the directors, convincing himself that it is the right decision. The Training Manager accepts the new task of producing the timetable, but reinforces the workload he has, by adding the word 'somehow'. This is recognised, but the importance of the work is reinforced, along with the tight but realistic timescales.

The last part of the interview is a negotiation and both parties have gained and conceded points. The Personnel Manager has accepted the delay, but forced a time for the report to be delivered. The Training Manager has had the problem of his workload recognised, the delay in the appraisal report agreed, but his workload is still heavier than he would ideally like.

After the interview we talked with both parties. The Personnel Manager had been reasonably pleased with the way the meeting had gone. The Training Manager had found the beginning of the meeting frustrating, as he had been prevented from presenting his whole case.

The Personnel Manager's comments

When we had finished reviewing the last few weeks work and moved on to think about the next six weeks, I knew the interview was going to be difficult.

We have a heavy workload at the moment in the department, and Joe is no exception. The difficulty is that Joe does tend to be a bit long-winded. I knew that if I simply asked him what work he had on, he would give me a complete list, full of detail, to prove to me how busy he was. Not only is this time-consuming, but at the end I can never remember all the details anyway.

I do not mean to imply that he is a major problem for me. He is very good at his job and is valued throughout the company. He is very skilful at presenting ideas and linking them together. I suppose that comes from his job, and he is frequently used by the other managers when they have presentations to make, to check their ideas. The trouble is he does tend to over-rely on that approach, and getting him to give a short answer is hard. The only way I know is to ask specific questions and, if necessary, interrupt him, when I have another question.

In retrospect, I think I should have let him know that I knew how busy he was. I sensed, and I suppose I should have realised, that he would try to justify his heavy workload. That was unnecessary, as I agreed with that, but how was he to know, if I didn't tell him? Also I should have let him have his say, and then pick up the details. Certainly if he had started going in to too much detail, I would then have had to get him to give me a general picture, but I probably could have managed that.

However, the short specific questions worked. It was obvious he had not thought through all the details, and there was no way I was going to agree to postponing or delaying anything until that was done.

Overall I think it was a successful meeting. I know he was not completely happy at the end about the timescales on the appraisal report. But I feel I cannot let that slip more than the month I agreed. I know the timescale is tight, so I will keep a close eye on that to see if he needs any help.

The Training Manager's comments

Going into the interview I had felt very pressurised by work, and I was determined to tell my boss about the difficulties. It seemed to me that he had been overloading me recently, and that I could not do anything properly.

I wanted to tell him about the whole workload. Without that, it was difficult to explain why I had a problem, and not to sound simply as though I was complaining. He wanted to get into the detail immediately, and I found it quite frustrating. Every time I tried to expand the conversation, he narrowed it down, and sometimes cut me off when I tried to explain something. He even seemed to be making light of the work, suggesting at one point that my secretary, Pauline, could deal with something which I saw as important.

Gradually, though, I got out the whole picture, and then his probing questions helped me to sort things out. When he began to push me to be specific about the number of hours involved, that helped me to think it through for myself. The same thing happened when he began to ask me about how many managers I planned to see. I had not really thought about it before, and that was helpful.

In the end I felt he was wrong to push so hard to get the work done on the appraisal, but at least I knew what was expected of me and that was helpful.

INTERVIEW BETWEEN A MANAGEMENT SERVICES
MANAGER AND A SUBORDINATE

The Management Services Manager has called the meeting with a senior member of his staff. The subordinate is currently working on three projects: an investigation of new packaging materials and methods, a study of waste to check reclamation and recycling and an initial investigation into the possible application of office automation within the company. He is an experienced and conscientious member of the department, who is used to working and managing large projects with comparatively little supervision.

Manager: Thank you for coming to see me, Ken. I wanted to raise a slight problem with you. I'm conscious of the fact that you've got these three projects on packaging, on waste and the office information one. What I've noticed is that your head's down all the while, and you're clearly working very hard on it. They're three big pieces of work. But I think you should know that the feedback I'm picking up from the directors, who are interested in the projects, and the Production Manager, who is interested in the packaging, is they're wondering where you've got to.

At first sight this appears to be a statement of purpose, but, in fact, is only giving the subordinate information. This, though, is helpful and the admission that he has clearly been working hard and that the projects are large is liable to set the subordinate at his ease so he is less defensive. The manager feeds back the directors' reaction. This is a statement: there is no question and the manager waits for the subordinate to respond.

Subordinate: Oh dear. Well, it is difficult. There's an awful lot of work in all three projects, that's the problem. They want me to provide them with good analysis. There's an awful lot of information I've got to get, before I can give that to them. I don't really know where to start, because I'm trying to carry all three of them at once, that's the trouble. It would be all right if it was one at a time but …

Manager: What sort of problems do they give you?

The manager probes to make the response more specific.

Subordinate: Well, it's trying to carry all three things at once is difficult in itself. There are some real problems in the sense of actually getting information I want, and the more information I get on some of it, the more I have difficulty in deciding what to do

about it, and I'm a bit loathe to feedback to the managers incomplete or inaccurate information. I feel really sort of stuck, I suppose.
Manager: Stuck on what to do next, or stuck on what to tell them?

The manager uses the subordinate's words to frame the question. This is a specific question to separate the project work from reporting on progress.

Subordinate: Stuck on what to tell them. I know they want some feedback. I know they want to know what's happening and so on, but short of telling them that I've got a lot more work to do, I don't quite know what to do, you know.
Manager: Have you told them anything?

The manager is maintaining control through asking questions. In this short sequence he goes from an open question to a specific question and finally a closed question to check out an assumption that he has made.

Subordinate: Well, no, I don't suppose I have really. That's probably why you're getting the feedback you're getting. The trouble with the waste is that George wants his information now really. He's under pressure to look at ways of getting some money in, if you like, in the department, and he's quite right, I'm sure, that probably if we can find the right way of either recycling or selling the waste more effectively, that would be to his benefit. I understand why he wants it but, you see, we set up a system or set up some equipment for recycling waste and at the same time we enter this packaging project, and if I can't get some results that say we should go for some different sort of packaging, then we won't want the system that I might recommend for recycling the waste.

The subordinate admits that he has fed back nothing and starts to explain why.

Manager: So is it only packaging waste that you have been considering?
Subordinate: Well, it's primarily that, to be honest. There is some material recycling.
Manager: So, how far have you got on that? I understand the connection between the packaging and the waste project. How far have you got on with the other waste?
Subordinate: I must say, that's not an area I've looked at in great depth at the moment. Because of the work that I've been doing on the packaging, I've been tending to link it with the packaging project and then umm ...
Manager: I understand that. I mean, in one sense, that seems quite

sensible. I suppose the consequence of that, inevitably, is that you can't finish the waste project, any of it, until you finish ...

Subordinate: Until you've done the work on the packaging you see.

Manager: But that's not wholly true, is it, in terms of the other sorts of waste? You could look at the material.

Here the manager is checking out the assumption that nothing can be done on the waste project, until the packaging has been decided.

Subordinate: I could do that. That would only be a minor bit of it, I think. The problem is with the packaging.

Manager: Are you saying you don't think that George would understand you can't do the packing waste, until you've made the decision on the type of packaging?

The manager is still maintaining control through asking questions. It is becoming increasingly clear his concern is with feeding back information on the projects, rather than concern about the projects' progress. He refers back to George and challenges the subordinate's implicit assumption that George will not understand the connection between the waste and packaging projects.

Subordinate: Well, I don't think he'd be interested. I think he wants it now, you know.

Manager: Yes, well, he's got the waste now.

Subordinate: I know. Yeah. At the moment, my fear is tackling the big problem about recycling packaging. We're going to need new machinery, a new system to operate it, and then we'll probably go, from what little bit I know, to a totally different packaging anyway. It would be madness to invest in new equipment now, when we could want something totally different in the near future.

Manager: Presumably George would understand that too?

The manager ignores the emotive statements 'totally different' and refocuses on George's reaction by using a closed question.

Subordinate: Yes, I suppose he would, but I must say, sometimes he behaves as if he doesn't, you know. He says 'I don't care, I want it set up now.' As you say, he's got the problem now, hasn't he?

Manager: Now, why do you think he's behaving like that?

Subordinate: Well, I suppose he's being kicked by his boss isn't he, to get a better constant saving out of the material waste?

Manager: Well, in terms of the work you're doing on this, I understand the connection between the packaging and waste projects and that you've got to sort out some priorities. At least concentrate on that in the short term. You give me the impression that you're doing a bit of this and a bit of that and that you're getting nowhere fast.

It is unclear why the manager does not continue to explore the reasons for George's behaviour. This might have been more helpful in getting the subordinate to understand George's position. Instead the manager summarises briefly and feeds back an impression he has formed.

Subordinate: Well, the problem is that I keep going to the packaging people, and they're all enthusiastic. They come and see me and they give me information and so on, but when you get down to the specifics they haven't got it. They've got to go away and research it themselves. Then they've got to come back. And you find the suppliers give you a bit of information, but not enough. Then I've got to remember what I'm working on, the recycling project, and particularly the word processor project, which I'm also trying to do, to follow that up. Every time you check it out, it takes another few days or up to a week or more to get a reply. I'm really dependent on these guys supplying me with the information. It sounds like I'm complaining but I don't mean to do that. But I need a bit more information all the time, and I need a bit more information before I can give the management a sensible answer.
Manager: So, what's stopping you then? This concern about — what do you mean by a sensible answer?

The manager asks a multiple question. The first question does not lead on from the subordinate's comments. The second question uses the subordinate's words and is much more powerful.

Subordinate: That's the problem. I don't feel that until I get a bit more information and I can get a feel about what the options are in packaging terms, both materials and equipment, that I can provide the management with any indicators that are sensible, you know?
Manager: When you picked up the word processor project, which was the last one we picked out, we talked about workload and whether we thought you could manage it and the time-scales which were actually quite long on that one.

Having asked the question 'What is a sensible answer?' and not really received an answer, the manager has a choice. Does he pursue the question or does he try another way to get the subordinate's view? Certainly, at this stage, it is unclear why he has raised the subject of timescales.

Subordinate: They are on that one. Yeah. I wouldn't expect it to happen for a couple of years.

Manager: I suppose what I'm concerned about is this feeling that you don't want to go back until you've almost got a solution to present to them. I don't think that's the need. What they're worried about is that you're actually not doing anything. I've obviously told them that you're working hard and so on, but you seem to be saying that you don't want to go back until you've got something to say – positive about some solution. Whereas what they're starting to say is that they want to know what the hell is happening. I know from some of the conversations we've had that the quality of the work you've done is good so far.

This is good. The manager is confronting the subordinate, that his view of what should be fed back is at variance with his clients' views and needs. Their expectations are less than the subordinate supposes.

The sequence of these statements, however, could be improved. The final point recognising the 'quality of the work' is helpful: it stresses that the issue for the manager is 'feedback', not the work that has been done, recognising the contributions the subordinate has made. It would be better though if this was mentioned earlier; to finish with it lessens the impact of the differing views and potentially allows the subordinate to continue on the issue of quality.

Subordinate: Well, it is coming, you know. It just seems a bit daft to go to them with half-baked information, doesn't it? The word processing isn't even …
Manager: Why is it half-baked?
Subordinate: Well, because I haven't got all the information I need to really indicate what to do.
Manager: So, it's incomplete? Half-baked?
Subordinate: Yeah. That's right.

The subordinate starts with an emotional appeal, a 'bit daft' and 'half-baked'. The manager maintains control using an open question, based on the subordinate's words, followed by a closed question to distinguish between incomplete and half-baked.

Manager: Are you worried that they won't recognise that it is incomplete?
Subordinate: Yeah, because they're under pressure to do things now, so they'll grab hold of whatever seems to be the best option with the limited information I can give them. That's what worries me.

Manager: What you're saying is that, if it looks like a half-baked solution, your fear is that they'll jump for that rather ...

Subordinate: Yeah. Anything is better than nothing, and I don't want to ...

Manager: So, is there another way you can present information on progress without them necessarily jumping to a false conclusion?

The manager does not accept that the problem is solely the clients jumping to conclusions, and he starts to investigate how to feed back information.

Subordinate: I suppose so, yes, I could but ...

Manager: You don't want to.

This is a difficult decision for the manager: should he pick up the obvious reticence of the subordinate or should he continue to concentrate on what could be done? He is probably right to confront the reticence, but he must not forget the possible actions and must return to them. On the other hand he could continue with a question like 'Good, so how do you think it could be presented?' If this is done, the manager must beware of producing a logical, rational course of action for the subordinate, to which he has no commitment. In the end the reticence will have to be confronted.

Subordinate: No. It worries me that they'll start putting me under pressure to do something now, before I've got all the information. So you think that I should start to feed the information back and do it carefully, so that even if it's incomplete at least they'll feel something's happening?

The subordinate feeds back what the manager has been saying.

Manager: Well, I think it's important they recognise that something is happening. Yes. I suppose what I'm concerned about is this notion you have about the worry of going back with something incomplete. But I can't see that the people you would be going back to wouldn't recognise that it was incomplete. Are you concerned that if it was incomplete, they would think it was a shoddy piece of work?

It is not clear what purpose the manager is working on at this stage. Having got from the subordinate some recognition of the problem, this would be the time to move on to 'how and what should be fed back', helping the subordinate to avoid his fears that the managers and directors would jump to conclusions. However, it appears that the manager is moving on to a general concern of how the subordinate works with his employers. This may be a concern that the manager now has, but it would be more appropriate to raise it at another meeting or after the specific purpose of this meeting is finished.

Subordinate: No, I don't think I am. I think my worry is more about the fact they won't be interested in its incompleteness. They'll actually be pressing me to say 'Well, come on, do it now. It doesn't matter that you haven't done all the work, all the research, but that you give us your decision now. That's all we want.' And they'll go for a quick answer. They've done it before, haven't they? They go for a piece of equipment because they're under pressure to do something now and six months, nine months later you get more information and they say 'Really, you shouldn't have done that. You should be handling this other piece of equipment.' I know you can't hang on for ever waiting for information, because things are always changing anyway but – I recognise that – but, it does seem to me, that in this area of packaging there are a number of options and I don't have all the information. I don't even have the range of it that would help to make the decision now, which is what they want to do. You're right. What I've been doing is avoiding giving them information, so that they can even make the choice, because if they do they'll certainly go for the wrong choice. I'll get blown up six months down the line because I should have known it, and perhaps I should. It's like Catch 22. I don't feel at the moment that's a good decision, but six months later they'll almost certainly think it's a bad decision.

Manager: It's not your decision, is it?

Subordinate: No, but they won't see it like that, will they? They'll see it's my advice that led them to make their decision.

Manager: I must admit that I find this a bit difficult to understand in a way, because you sound like you're saying 'I don't feel I can go back to give them a progress report, because I haven't finished and, therefore, even if it's blatantly obvious I haven't finished, they'll take a decision. I'd rather wait until I've got the perfect decision.'

Subordinate: No, that's not true. It's too strong. I don't mean that at all. I just feel that they're under a lot of pressure to make a decision.

By generalising the issue the manager has achieved little. The subordinate restates his point of view, only at more length and more strongly. This makes the manager overstate his own views and the exchanges, having started with the germ of an agreement, end with a disagreement.

Manager: Which would you like to concentrate on?
Subordinate: Well, I feel that if I could get the packaging project into a reasonable state, and I don't mean complete, I mean so I feel I can survey the field reasonably well ...

This elicits a more reasonable response from the subordinate.

Manager: How long is that going to take?
Subordinate: Don't know. Because I'm finding it so difficult to get information out of the suppliers. That's the trouble.
Manager: When will you know that you've surveyed the field adequately?
Subordinate: Well the last time I looked at it, I actually identified the main areas − we had talked about the board, we had talked about polystyrene, we had talked about shrink wrappings and so on. Then I went back into the options and I feel I haven't got all the information. When I've got enough information on each of the main fields, then it'll be OK. It's the styrenes at the moment that are bloody awful; the suppliers ... I don't know why. You would have thought they'd have been keen. I can't get the information. I can't get it in a sensible form anyway. Once I've got that, I'm quite happy for the management to have their first preliminary report.

The manager is now back in control. Again this is achieved, not by using his presenting skills, but by asking questions.

Manager: So, what you're actually saying is that you really can't do much more on the waste until you've decided on ...
Subordinate: Yeah. I think it would be very unwise because of the ...
Manager: So, what are you going to do with George, who's responsible for waste then?

Having clarified how the subordinate wants to continue to tackle the work, the manager brings the interview back to feeding back information to the other managers by asking a question.

Subordinate: I suppose I'd better go and see him and talk to him about what the position is.
Manager: What are you going to do with the packaging?
Subordinate: I don't know. What I ought to do is fend him off for another week or two. Hopefully, I'll have more information, enough ...
Manager: How are you going to fend him off?
Subordinate: I ought to go to him and explain to him what I'm explaining to you now − why I'm not responding, rather than give

him any information, because I'm bloody sure if I give him the information he would switch now. That would be mad.

Again the use of questions to draw this part of the interview to a conclusion. The subordinate does not appear to have modified his views at all, but at least he agrees to explain the situation to George.

Manager: What about the other one? What about the office automation? That's the boss's pet interest.

The manager moves on to the next part of the interview. There is no summarising of the actions the subordinate will take before the change of subject. A short summary would be better: this would demonstrate an agreement on the actions and a finishing of the subject, and hence a joint recognition that the interview can move on.

Subordinate: I know, I know.
Manager: That's a long timescale.
Subordinate: That's a long timescale. I don't understand why a manager at that level can't actually see that it's a long timescale project.
Manager: He can.
Subordinate: Then why is he pressing for some information now? I've been to IBM, I've been to Bull, I've been to Norsk Data, I've been to Datamax and I've …
Manager: He's not expecting an answer. He just wants to know.

The subordinate seems to react to the phrase 'pet interest', and appears to express some frustration at the director 'pressing for some information now'.

Subordinate: So, what are you suggesting? I just give him an interim report on what I'm doing?
Manager: Yes.
Subordinate: Is he going to be happy with that?
Manager: I think he's realistic. I don't know how much information you've collected, but some of that information may well alter his opinion about some of his ideas so far. I mean, he's not asking you to come up with a 'be all and end all' solution. If you come up with one solution, he's going to quiz you all over the place anyway. It's really very much a trawl, isn't it?

Now the subordinate has started to ask questions and the manager is providing the information. The manager's question is rhetorical.

Subordinate: The whole idea is that terminals linked to the mainframe is better than the standard PCs around the office.

Manager: But it wasn't at the beginning. The director's ideas were for using cheap PCs for applications in terms of office automation.

Subordinate: I suppose, in some ways, it's got similarities with packaging things, as if you really go through office automation – I suppose this is the thing I'm beginning to discover – that it's so much bigger than word processing, because you really want it linked to a whole range of things, don't you? I'm restricting myself at the moment to – my focus is in terms of advantages of word processing on the mainframe as distinct from word processors. Everytime I get information, because everyone else is trying to tell you, especially the suppliers, it raises new questions.

Manager: Of course.

Subordinate: And there's a lot of information. A lot of the ideas are very good and I'm sure will be very useful, but umm ...

Manager: I suppose there's two elements in this. It's a bit like your packaging thing in the sense that, because the application is moving at an enormous rate, if you wait, something else will be on the market which might be even better.

Subordinate: It's even worse, isn't it?

Manager: Then you wait for ever.

Subordinate: You wait for ever. I mean, I know that, that office information. There is just an endless stream of stuff. Somewhere along that line you know jolly well you're just going to have to take all the information you've got and make a decision. I haven't got that far with that one at all. That's really a matter of just trying to understand a little bit of what's in the field.

The manager is now using different skills to gain information from the subordinate; he gives information himself and waits for the response. This is reinforced by encouraging responses such as 'of course' and 'then you wait for ever'. The purpose of the interview has shifted, the manager appears to be working to ensure that both he and the subordinate have the same view of the project. Hence he introduces his own view of the director's interest.

Manager: You know that he's interested in computing? You picked up on things that would actually get his interest. You sound like you are loading yourself with defining this piece of work as coming up with a proposal for something or other.

Subordinate: I thought that's what he wanted. He specified it in costs and, therefore, wanted a proposal.

Manager: I think that's true, but it's an input into his thinking about what policy we should have ... I think you're right about things moving fast. If we chose one solution for word processing, you don't want it then restricting your options for other applications.

Subordinate: I would have thought you wanted something that linked word processing, communication, with certainly E-mail and electronic diaries. It's got to be all the same – linked with all the other systems that we use as well.

Manager: So, you can't make an analysis producing a simplistic cost comparison between doing the word processing and other methods.

Subordinate: Does he want to make a big change? I mean, will it link with the next generation of computers?

Manager: I don't think he's thought that far in advance.

The process of both sharing what the director needs and thinks continues. In comparison with earlier stages of the interview, both are talking equally and the emphasis is on opinions.

Manager: Look I think it's potentially an enormous enquiry. But more importantly, his thinking is likely to be developing. It is his favourite subject, God alone knows what he's reading and thinking now. I think it would be best if you went and saw him to update him on what you've done so far. Not only because he's asked what you've been doing, but probably, more importantly, for you to find out what his current views are. It would be a complete waste for you to carry on some line of enquiry, only to find out later that he's moved on and already discounted that idea.

Subordinate: OK, that sounds sensible, so long as he doesn't expect too much.

Manager: I'll have a word with him and tell him that you're still collecting general information. OK?

Subordinate: Yeah. OK.

Manager: Good.

The Management Services Manager's Comments

Ken is one of my most experienced project consultants. I was somewhat concerned about the feedback I was getting that he was getting nowhere fast on these projects. I needed to find out if this was true, or if there was some other reason for these comments.

I quickly found out that the waste and packaging projects were connected. Also that he had done a lot of work. But on exploring this further, I found I had two possible problems. First getting him to feed back his progress and second this unrealistic concern about the need for completeness of this work and connected with that his

understanding of his clients' needs. I know from his point of view
they are the same issue, but for me they are different: one is to do
with how you feed back, the other is the way the role is defined, its
limits and the sort of relationship you try and need to establish.

I decided to concentrate on the question of feedback. I tried to do
this by questioning him and to get him to see the situation from the
client's point of view. I hope in the process of doing this, I did not
criticise his work. I tried to demonstrate that I understood and
agreed with the connections between his projects and recognised it
would be inappropriate to complete the waste project before deciding on the packaging. I think this reassured him that I thought the
quality of his work was good, but he still needed to keep the clients
informed.

The second part of the discussion was very useful. I realised his
view of the project was different from mine and I was able to tell
him what I knew. In the end we were both clearer about the project
and the need to keep in touch with the director and his thinking.

At the end I think he will go back and tell his clients what the
status of the projects is. It's not my style to give someone of Ken's
level and experience an instruction. I do not think it's necessary,
which is why I got him to see for himself that he had to keep them
informed. I am sure enough was said for him to get the message. But
I shall certainly ask him in a couple of days how things are going.

I still need to think about this other possible problem of how he
sees his role.

The Project Consultant's Comments

I was not surprised when my boss wanted to see me about the state
of my projects. I've had difficulty collecting the information, and the
two projects being interrelated has not helped.

As a boss, he is one of the better ones I've had. He tends to trust
you and leave you alone. His philosophy is to give you a project
and let you decide how to do it, judging you by your results. I do
not mean he is uninterested in you or your methods, he is, but he
trusts your expertise and knowledge and your ability to manage
projects.

In terms of this interview, I got a very clear steer I've got to go
and see these people quickly. I know he will check to see if I have,
also to see if I need any help or support from him.

What did I like about the interview? Firstly he checked what I had
done. He understood and recognised two of the projects were
interrelated. He never said that he thinks my work is not good, or

that I have not been working hard on these projects. He recognised that because of their nature I had a problem on what and how to feed back. But he stressed the clients still needed feed-back. In principle, that was easy for me to agree with and accept. His lack of criticism meant that I did not feel defensive.

His questioning also helped as it forced me to think and accept the client's needs, rather than concentrating on my own difficulties. Of course, rationally I know that is what one should do, but when you are in the situation it sometimes gets out of perspective. His raising the issue, but not pushing too far, was good. It let me know there were concerns, without patronising me or lecturing me about it.

The discussion on office automation was most helpful for both of us. It clarified the position, because we shared what we knew. My view of the project is now different and I do not have a problem in going to see the director to update him.

On the down side, I think he overreacted to my comments about not having enough information to provide answers for George. It's easy for him, at his level. He does not get the pressure I get. He knows that, but knowing is different from having to deal with it. We will have to talk about this at some time, as he seems to think I want to provide all the answers and have nice tidy complete projects before I go back to the clients – and that is not true.

I've been putting off going back in the hope that the next piece of information will give me enough. I know now I can't wait any longer, and that's helpful.

INTERVIEW BETWEEN A SALESMAN AND HIS AREA MANAGER

This is a monthly interview between a salesman and his regional sales manager. This interview should be seen in connection with the data discussed in the chapter on 'Managing Change'.

Manager: Well, here we are looking at your six months' figures. I thought it would be a good idea to – in addition to a review in June – to look forward to the next six months, because, as you know, we've got some fairly elaborate plans for the autumn and leading up to Christmas. Now is the time to study in a little bit more depth the strengths and weaknesses of any problems you're facing and really to set ourselves some objectives for the next few months. What do you say about that?

This is a general statement of purpose, outlining what will be discussed and setting the discussion in the context of the year's work.

Salesman: That sounds very good, David. Sounds fine.

Manager: Good. Well, I suppose overall June was not a bad month for you. I have to say that, in terms of overall company performance, yours was one of the better ones. However, I suppose, against that encouraging background, one tends to concentrate perhaps on some of the weaker areas. What about the cake section? How do you feel you've fared with that this month?

The manager sets the scene for concentrating on the weaker performance areas. The praise that precedes this is somewhat grudging: it is not 'June was a good month', but 'June was not a bad month for you'.

Salesman: Well, I think I've done all right. It's hard work.

Manager: The continuing problems of keeping the shelf space, I suppose.

This is not easy for the manager, because it is clearly a subject that has been discussed on previous occasions. It is, therefore, important to demonstrate that the manager is aware of the problem, but he does not want to lead the salesman too much and in the process ignore or miss other problems in the cake market. At this stage, a more neutral comment to promote and encourage more information from the salesman, would be better.

Salesman: Well, I think it is about keeping the shelf space. Our product range isn't the most up-to-date. It's the most competitive market for our products. It's the one where 'own brands' mean much more. I have to keep going round to ensure that our products are still on the shelf, but every time I go round to make sure it is still kept on the shelf, the amount that has been sold is very little. But, I do know that if we lost the shelf space, then there's no hope whatsoever of getting it back. I think our range is a bit – basically, it's what it was twenty years ago and in this region ... Perhaps in other parts of the country they do better, but in this region you find all the fancy German chocolate cakes and things like that, which sell a hell of a lot more than our things do.

Manager: Well, slightly different sort of market that perhaps. A little bit voguish. At least with ours, they're a steady seller. I think the market overall, as we've said, is somewhat static. Its probably a great challenge to the marketing department to see if they can come up with some new initiative. I think on the basis that it is not an easy market, and I do accept the hard graft you have to go through, your results are encouraging but we must keep at that one.

The manager says the German chocolate cake is in a different market to refocus the interview on to their own products. The recognition of the salesman's efforts is useful. However, it is unclear at the end of his statement whether he wants to continue discussing the cake market or to change the subject. If he wants to continue, a question would be helpful; otherwise a more detailed summary then the introduction of a new topic.

Salesman: Well, I'm reasonably pleased with it. I think, as I say, it really is hard work. I don't feel as though they're falling over themselves to get the next batch of cherry cakes or ginger cakes, but at least ours seem to be holding up better than some. I think the quality of our products is, in the main, not bad and from our point of view we've not suffered. I mean, we are suffering because the market is pretty static but we're not suffering because our products aren't as good or anything. In that sense, I think that's probably the only reason we keep the shelf space, because some of our competitors are hardly selling anything.

Manager: I think my only thought on cakes is whether there might be an area for developing some more personalised promotions for some of your outlets, if we feel that they've got a reasonable volume. Maybe the product could bear having a sticker on it, and we could actually produce something that is specific to that particular shop – exclusively for that particular outlet for a limited period. Clearly, we haven't got a tremendous amount of resources to put behind it, but targeting it in that way may be more useful. I don't know if you have any thoughts on that?

The manager maintains control of the interview, by using his presenting skills to introduce the new idea of personalised promotion. Unfortunately, he does not comment on the points the salesman makes about the quality of their products. The danger with this is that he can create the feeling that he is not listening to the salesman, even ignoring his views. If the manager does not want to discuss the quality issue, it would still be better to make a comment such as, 'I'm glad to hear what you say about the quality of our products. I was wondering though if there might be an area for developing some more personalised ...'

Salesman: I haven't thought of that at all, but it could be useful at this time of the year because cakes aren't really a summer product. I

know that's taken account of in the targets, so that could be useful. I
wonder if it would be better though to keep that for the autumn.

Manager: Yes. It would take us a little time to get marketing to get
that organised.

Salesman: It always does, doesn't it?

Manager: We can get them to pull their finger out occasionally. I
think that would then give us a good platform for the autumn and
through to the Christmas period.

This is a nice example of where the manager demonstrates he has
heard the comments about the marketing department and in the
process dismisses it from the following discussion, continuing with
the point he wants to make.

Salesman: That's interesting that.

Manager: That's good. Now.

Salesman: You were thinking about some cards or posters that
they could stick up as well, weren't you?

Manager: I think we need to give them some form of material.

Salesman: Some merchandising material?

Manager: Yes.

Salesman: That could be quite useful.

Manager: That's fine. Now, let's turn to the biscuits and cookies
section. Perhaps deal with the main range of biscuits before we
move on to some of the newer items. There again, overall a
reasonable month, but you seem to have a particular weakness with
creams. That's odd because creams have been going reasonably well
with the company.

The manager makes a statement and waits for a response. This has a
similar effect to an open question, allowing the salesman to answer
in the way he wants.

Salesman: Really? I honestly can't explain that. I've no idea. No
idea at all. Nobody seems to be the least bit interested. It's not for
want of trying. I really don't understand that.

Manager: What's that? A price problem or the variety of creams?

The manager only gets a vague response to his statement and has to
probe further. However, his question is not good. It is better to take
each aspect of the problem one at a time. How do we compare with
the competition on price? Are the competitors' creams selling?
Why? Are there new varieties of creams on the market? In this way
the interviewer may help the salesman see connections between
information that he was previously unaware of. The general

questions will tell the manager what the salesman already knows and thinks, but take it no further.

Salesman: No, our prices are about the same as everybody else's. Perhaps, I don't know, perhaps it is our variety. There's certainly I think − no, I know what it was. Last month the other biscuit maker had a price cut on them, a special promotion. I did notice that places that would normally take them, didn't this month. They had theirs instead. They're not a popular biscuit round here, I don't think.

The manager now has a choice: does he pick up what the competition is doing or 'they're not a popular biscuit'?

Manager: I have, in fact, picked up one or two ...
Salesman: They've been down all year really. Last month was particularly bad.
Manager: I notice that one or two of the own label producers were producing what one might call sharper creams − lemon and lime − moving away from raspberry and blackcurrant. So perhaps there's a change in habit in terms of people wanting less sickly products.

In fact, the manager uses the 'popular biscuit' indirectly to introduce some new information about possible changes in taste. It is sensible to get the salesman's reaction to this, but premature; he should probe more on the cream problem to ensure he has all the information, before introducing his own ideas.

Salesman: That may be true, I suppose.
Manager: Perhaps that's another burden we're going to lay on marketing, but we'll see. It would be a shame, if your sales slipped too far behind target there. Well, let's turn in that range to the newer products.

The manager gets no real feedback on his ideas. It is difficult to know how powerful the statement, 'it would be a shame ...' is, as this would depend on their relationship. With some managers it would be very clearly an instruction to get sales up, others not. Similarly, some subordinates would read such a statement as an instruction, others would not even hear it. Whatever the relationship, it would be preferable to make it more positive, for instance, 'I would not like to see your sales slip too far behind target.'

Salesman: Right. Which one?
Manager: The luxury and the individual. How are you doing with the luxury? Have you got that into most of the accounts now?

One question at a time.

Salesman: Mmm. There was a certain sort of hesitancy about taking them, you know, whether the shelf life was as long as the others. But, given the time of the year, I think they've gone in quite well. They're a good biscuit.

Manager: We've got no own label competition presumably. I'm not aware of any serious competition.

These two statements would be better as questions. There is time for the manager to introduce his own view and perceptions later.

Salesman: Not own label, no, but most of the bigger supermarkets sell something which is rather similar. They tend to be imported products. I think the incentive is that there's a slightly higher profit margin. So, if they can sell one packet of those, they have twice as much in the tills as they got from a packet of digestive or creams or something.

Manager: Ah, that's interesting. You've made them aware of that?

Salesman: Oh, yes. They're definitely interested in that and, as I say, we're really the only ones of their normal callers that actually stock and sell them. As I say, some of the local supermarkets round here are stocking imported biscuits. I don't know where they're getting them from. Whether they import them themselves I don't know.

Manager: There are one or two specialist people who are bringing in more and more continental stuff.

Salesman: We're on our own, which is nice. I suppose the problem is going to be that if we build the market nicely, somebody else is going to come in, aren't they?

Manager: Well, that's always a challenge. Thinking forward then to autumn and obviously this product has particular reference to the Christmas period. In terms of incentives would it be sensible to think of increasing the profit margin for the retailer or doing something for the consumer? Our view at the moment is, that if you cut the price of a luxury product without undermining the value, for instance you might have an on-pack offer ... but, perhaps from what you say, it would be wise to think of some retail incentive.

The manager nicely shifts the emphasis from what has happened to the future. The input on the management's thinking on price is helpful, although it would be better if the question followed this statement, instead of preceding it.

Salesman: They've given it quite prominent displays. I thought the merchandising gear we had for the launch was very, very effective. I thought the green packaging really had that sense of quality about it. It had more the sort of feel of a box of chocolate's packaging than a biscuit packaging, and that can convey all sorts of things about the quality and so on. The product's good enough to stand the price, I think. Where it's gone particularly well is actually in the large town shops in the centre. I reckon a lot of people buy for work, for biscuits with coffee at work rather than stuff to take home. So, I guess for Christmas, what I think would be quite nice – I don't know whether the idea is any good – is to get them packaged up in tins for presents, you know. I don't think we should do too much. I certainly don't think we should do anything which would cheapen the image of the product. I'll have a word. It might be worthwhile, I mean the original launch displays have gone now – I would think that with the autumn coming up, it might be nice to have another display especially for autumn.

The discussion on the luxury biscuit is flowing better than when cakes and creams were the subject. This may be because the salesman feels more secure about his performance, but the manager is also stimulating the discussion. He is picking up the points the salesman makes, inputting information when required and asking for and listening to the salesman's opinions.

Manager: Now, to make that economically viable we would need a fairly substantial commitment across the country, and obviously from you as well. Do you feel you could get a special pack, say a special tin pack, into most of your accounts?
Salesman: I would think in December, yes. No, in most perhaps not. I think that's the sort of thing that would go in the larger town centre stores, where people pick up presents. But we might be able to get it into other places we're not supplying, such as present shops. There's a lot of gifty sort of shops now. You might be able to get it into the sort of … I don't know if that makes any sense.
Manager: Well, I think I understand, So, what we're really saying is that in town you've got an opportunity to get them displayed, a lot of customers, but if we can identify one or two perhaps even up-market shops … Well, that leads us on to the individual cookies, I think you will recall the strategy with these, entering into the confectionery/snack market, instant consumption, individual purchases, but very specifically aimed at getting us into new accounts to get us away from the traditional cake purchaser. Perhaps there I'm tempted to sneak a little bit of a forward look to the end of our review, and can we look at new accounts and closed accounts? It's gone the wrong way this month with you and I wonder whether

you're having the opportunity, really the time, to pursue new account opportunities for this line.

The manager takes up the salesman's ideas and feeds this back in terms of the level of commitment necessary to make the suggestion economically viable. The salesman agrees that in principle it would be possible to achieve these sales. Without knowing the details of the business, it is difficult to know whether this is an adequately detailed agreement at this stage. The manager then summarises and goes on to introduce the next topic. This is introduced well. The previously discussed strategy is mentioned, then explained, and is linked to the accounts opened and closed. Having pointed out that this has gone the wrong way, he finishes weakly by giving the salesman a ready-made excuse for failing. A simple question to explore the difference would be to give the manager information to make the judgement, rather than making an assumption.

Salesman: Not as much as I would want. I think the problem with the list of potential new accounts you sent us is that with this particular product, even if we get it in, then they'll only take that product. The chances of getting them to buy anything other than the cookie are pretty well zero. So I've tended to concentrate, I think, much more on looking for accounts that will develop and in the end take more than just the cookie.

The manager now has a problem: from what the salesman has said it appears that he may not understand the strategy. (As the new product was introduced to get into outlets which did not traditionally stock biscuits and cakes, to compete with confectionery, it is hardly surprising that most outlets are unwilling to take the company's other products.)

Manager: Have you managed to visit the shops on that list I gave you?
Salesman: Most of them. Yes.
Manager: And what sort of response did you get?
Salesman: Well, as I thought, most of them would be prepared to take a case of the mixed cookies and that was all.
Manager: And what was their response to the product?
Salesman: Oh, they thought it was good, only the volume doesn't seem enormous.
Manager: Do you think we should use confectionery wholesalers? Perhaps we ought to see if any of those are on the patch, as an opportunity to get in at that grass roots level.

Again the manager moves on, although the salesman's answers are rather general.

Salesman: I guess that might be the case. I know some of them would get a call only once a month, but in the confectionery trade they would probably call reasonably regularly and actually alter the position on the displays of products to try and push something like this. I think that's the problem. It might be easier if we made a slightly larger-range, product range. It would feel like we were selling Mars bars then. I understand, I think I understand why we're doing it. It seems to me to be quite a good opportunity. As I say, from our point of view it's hard work if the new accounts are likely to only stock one product. The wholesalers, that's true, they may well go through, I mean they may well go through specialist confectionery wholesalers, whereas we're very much geared up to the grocery trade.

The salesman has started thinking; he is identifying differences between his normal business and the way the new outlets operate.

Manager: I think what we probably need to do then, Martin, is to get more information into the confectionery market. I'm not so sure that I don't even have a view we might even be able to employ some broker merchandising system, because I believe in confectionery once you get a shelf space for a product like ours, and assuming of course that the product sells through, and I see no reason why it shouldn't, the price is equivalent to that chocolate bar you just mentioned.

The manager again brings in his own ideas of how to deal with the possible problems. While they may be good and useful ideas, they seem a little premature and run the risk of stopping the salesman from further thinking. This is particularly true, as the salesman had been talking about how products are merchandised as well as bought by the outlets. It would be helpful and would make the interview easier to control, if the manager separated these issues. Without this, there is the tendency for the interview to jump from one topic to another. When this happens it is possible for the two people to have a strong feeling of agreeing, but when asked, to have different views about what has been agreed. Conversely, it is possible for two people to know they disagree without knowing specifically what about.

The manager already has an idea that the salesman may have not wholly understood the strategy behind the new product. The salesman is also, not surprisingly, concerned with volume of sales. There is also a hint in his answers that he sees the new product as simply an extension to the current range, rather than an attempt to get into and create new markets. This reinforces the need for the manager to provide ways of thinking about the problem by his questioning and presenting skills, or the salesman is liable to provide new information, but continue thinking and acting in the same way.

Salesman: No, the product seems to sell well, when you get it in, and there seems to be some reluctance to display with the confectioneries rather than with the biscuits. I think we do need to think about the way we do our merchandising. Chocolate bars actually stack very deeply, you know. You can put them in the display racks with bright packaging and so on, and they fit in. Our individual biscuits aren't so easy. The boxes we've got them in, even though they open up, they're not – they don't look as neat and tidy and fit as well as theirs. What we need is a better on-counter racking system.

Manager: The packaging was quite thoroughly researched and I think most consumers' preference was to actually see the biscuit through the transparent packaging. But that does mean, of course, that you don't get the bright colour over solid print.

Again a question to elicit more information would be better. This would prevent the confusion of the salesman talking of packaging and display of boxes of biscuits, while the manager is talking of packaging of individual biscuits.

Salesman: No, I understand that and the individual packaging is all right. It's just that the display packet looks fine when they're full; you take three out and they start falling over. Whereas you get those racked chocolate bar stands, you take one off and it still looks fine. You can take two off. It's only when it's empty that it looks awful, whereas ours tend to fall over a bit and so on, and then they don't look so good.

Manager: It's an interesting comment. Perhaps we ought to have a bulk supply for the retailers to fill up from. That's interesting. I will dwell on that, but I'd like to come back, I think, to an autumn objective in terms of accounts on that one. Perhaps before we concentrate on that again, we could turn to the savoury area – the cheese biscuits. Again, a fairly steady performance. Undoubtedly what we're seeing here is another part of this move from sweet to savoury.

The manager demonstrates he has heard the points about the stacking of biscuits and moves on. It is not clear why he has gone on to cheese biscuits at this stage. The salesman is obviously interested in the topic, but the manager must balance this with achieving his purpose. After all, the purpose of the meeting is not to discuss the merchandising of biscuits.

Salesman: And from traditional to new ranges. We're desperately short of products.

The salesman's view differs slightly from the manager's.

Manager: In terms of different varieties?
Salesman: Yes. Crackers — bread and butter I know — we churn them out and I know we make nice money out of them, but they are the same as bread and butter. I know everybody always stocks crackers, but what we need, I reckon now, is a mixed pack.
Manager: All I can say to you is that we're doing a lot of work in this area. Part of the concept is to capitalise on the 'healthy living' area, and as far as I understand, although it's still fairly early days, they're also looking at individual products that could go along with the individual biscuits, so we'd have a sweet and savoury individual snack line.

It is now clear why the savoury and cheese biscuits were discussed, as the manager has linked them with the individual biscuit. This is good skill, although the consequence at this stage of the interview is to curtail discussion on the cheese biscuits.

Salesman: Ah, that's interesting.
Manager: So, I think it's very important to persevere with this whole area which, of course, brings me back then to this opportunity to expand the range — to really research the opportunity to open new accounts, particularly accounts in this whole snack area. I think by expanding the range in this way we overcome that earlier thought you had that we haven't got a big enough range to achieve a substantial order from any one outlet.
Salesman: Well, I think that's the problem, yes.

It is unclear following the manager's comments, what the salesman has heard. At the start, the salesman is interested in the idea of a new product to supplement the individual biscuit. The manager does not start by talking about this: he ends by trying to reassure the salesman on this topic; in between, he stresses the importance of new accounts. The problem with this sequence is that the new accounts issue can be lost, as the salesman is still concerned with the product range.

It would be better to reassure him, and then stress the importance of the new accounts. The choice of language also weakens the impact of the statements. It would be more powerful to omit the 'I think's.

Manager: Now, in terms of the sort of confectionery, newsagent, tobacconist outlets on your patch, you said you had visited most on the list I gave you. You also were going to try and identify other possible outlets, which were not on the list. How did you get on there?

Salesman: Of course, there's a staggering number of them. The sort of shops I've called on have tended to be ones that I already know, because they're either next door to grocers or in the same shopping precinct. I have tried the odd thing like the odd garage and so on, when I stop and buy the petrol. There is an interest, you know, but as I say, they take one pack off me and that would be it. They're not really what I would call an account. If I had a couple of boxes in the back of the car I could probably sell them quite easily.

Manager: I think we've got to take this quite methodically.

In other words the manager thinks the salesman has not been methodical.

Salesman: Yeah.

Manager: I think what I would then like to consider with you is perhaps helping you by having maybe a mail shot that we could send to these accounts. We would obviously have to work out the number we would send to, because I'd like you to follow up the mail shot quite quickly with an actual face to face meeting. So obviously we can't blitz the lot, otherwise you'd be rushing round and not giving it enough attention.

Salesman: I'd guess there's more outlets like that.

Manager: I think that when we look at it we are going to find quite a few, so we may have to draw up a priority list of how many you think you can handle each day and each week and draw up a target plan. So perhaps in the next four weeks you can give some thought to that. That may even mean that you'll prune some of your existing accounts, because if they're very small and business is dropping off, you can afford to lose those, providing we can ensure that we replace them with better accounts. So, I think they're the sort of objectives.

Salesman: I understand what you mean. I suppose the problem I fear about dropping some of the existing accounts is that, if we replace them as a result of this research and the mail shots with accounts which are much nearer the tobacconist/newsagent outlet, then inevitably we might be able to generate a certain amount of cash from them, but it would detrimentally affect the cake market, because there is no way we could get those shops to take cake.

In this part of the interview the manager introduces a number of ideas – a mail shot, priority list, target plan and pruning some of the existing accounts. He chooses to present them as a sequence to give the salesman the complete picture from mail shots through to changing some accounts. This approach has the advantage that the salesman would understand the overall situation, but leaves the manager unsure of the salesman's reaction to the individual ideas. The manager would therefore have to go back and deal with items separately.

The alternative is to take one idea at a time. For instance, taking mail shots, is it a good idea? What should be in it? How long should the gap be between the outlet receiving it and the salesman's visit? Only when these issues have been explored, understood and agreed, would you go on to the next stage – who should they be sent to? This approach has the obvious advantage that it builds on common and shared understanding, but has the disadvantage that in this case the salesman does not know where it is leading.

Which would be the best approach in this interview? As we discussed in the chapter on Managing Change, some people prefer the whole picture, while others have a preference for an incremental approach. However, in this situation, apart from the personal preference of the salesman, there is another important factor. We already know that the salesman is concerned about the snack outlets and the limited range of product they will stock. Therefore, he will be highly sensitive, possibly even resistant, to the idea of substituting some of his existing accounts with new snack outlets. By the manager introducing the ideas in the way he has, it is almost certain that the salesman will hear the comments on changing outlets more powerfully than the other ideas, even to the extent of forgetting or not remembering the other points. In this situation it would, therefore, be better to take the argument point by point.

However, having got the predictable reaction, with the salesman linking the account issue to the static cake market, what should the manager do? He must demonstrate that he has heard the salesman's concern, and then return to the mail shot.

Manager: Well, that's obviously something we're going to have to consider very hard, because we've agreed that although it's not desperately exciting, we really must keep that cake business going. That's very important.

This is fine as far as it goes, but to wait for a reaction and not bring the interview back to the mail shot and snack outlets, runs the risk of allowing the salesman to control the topics discussed.

Salesman: Are there any new ideas about introducing new cakes? When we look at our biscuit range — I suppose it's about ten years ago we introduced the new chip range. We've got the luxury range and the individual biscuits as well, whereas the cakes really have been a very similar product range for as long as I've been with the company. Some new sort of cakes — I don't know what they could be.

Manager: The difficulty we have is that our range is the longer life cake. There's obviously an opportunity in the luxury shorter life market, as we perhaps mentioned earlier on with these chocolate specialities, but they're going to be difficult. I believe what is being examined, and we might share some thoughts on that, is moving to one or two traditional recipes, in fact, because that's very much part of appreciation of old fashioned things. We're looking at spice ranges again. Yes, I think in that area people are basically eating less cakes. It's always going to be a difficult one.

Not only is the manager answering the salesman's questions and points, but he is also introducing new information and ideas. The discussion on mail shots for the individual biscuit and prioritising accounts has disappeared.

It would have been more appropriate to introduce these points on cake developments, when cakes were being discussed earlier in the interview. However, the manager would have had to be careful, as the discussion is now about the cake market, not the performance of the salesman in the cake market. In this sense it is difficult to know what the purpose of the interview is at this stage. This is largely because the salesman is in control of what is discussed. Not surprisingly, he is liable to concentrate on subjects which reinforce the difficulties that exist in selling the company's products.

Salesman: I suppose they are eating slightly less cake. Certainly you go round the supermarket the shelf space is still quite large, but the sort of products we sell are starting to be in the corner rather than in the main.

Manager: Yes, that's worrying isn't it — to get out of the mainstream display areas.

Salesman: You're right. There's a number of them now where the more traditional sorts of products are being sold. Are we going to do Christmas puddings this year?

Another new subject, again introduced by the salesman.

Manager: Yes, we are. Traditional recipe cakes also, so that will obviously be one of the targets for the autumn again. Good. OK. Well, unless you've got anything else?

An offer to finish this stage of the interview.

Salesman: No, no. I'll think about the ideas, particularly about the luxury biscuits, and see if there are any ideas I come up with. I'll think about what shops might take them.

Manager: I'll also get this research done in terms of confectionery wholesalers.

Salesman: Well, that would be helpful.

Manager: Because I think that might be a useful opportunity, mightn't it? If you concentrated perhaps on those ... In the main you've been concentrating on retail outlets, but with the confectioners, if we could find a number of wholesalers and in particular if they did have a regular van sale service – it might not quite be the merchandising that we're looking for, but if you can get sufficient outlets going, then we can even think of hiring a housewife to do some merchandising on a regular basis ourselves. I don't think that should be a difficult task at all, but we should have to have the distribution base of course to be able to justify that.

Salesman: That would be smashing. I still think that – certainly with the biscuits – we could do with a decent sort of display and dispenser sort of thing.

Manager: Very expensive, those sort of items. I think what we can't afford to do – I'd be very reluctant to see the retail price move up at this stage.

Salesman: It's a good product.

Manager: Oh yes. But if poor display is inhibiting it, then that's something to look at. As I say, I know that display units are hideously expensive.

Salesman: They are. That's the thing.

Manager: Yes indeed. Maybe we've got to think of some permanent display unit, which would be even more expensive initially, but provided that we could keep it there and replenish the stock that might be the answer. OK then, well let's go on, and I will talk through your next month's targets and I'll explain the couple of special promotions that we're running.

The offer to finish this stage of the interview is accepted by the salesman, who starts to summarise what he will do. The manager continues by saying what he will do. The result is a very partial summary, with the manager not emphasising the major activities he wants the salesman to concentrate on or the key points he wants the salesman to understand.

While it is true that the interview has not finished and the manager will have time to summarise these points, it would certainly be better to do it before going on to the monthly targets. Targets are important for salesmen and will particularly command their attention. The best approach is to use this attention, not compete with it as such, but get the ideas understood and reinforce this understanding by using the targets.

The Sales Manager's Comments

Martin is a good salesman and he tends to hit his targets more times than not. He is very target-orientated, and his major motivation seems to be the increased self-esteem and the financial bonuses he receives when he meets his targets.

He is also loyal to his customers. I think this comes from the fact that over time he builds a good relationship and he makes sure that he repays any of the little favours he receives. Certainly in a couple of his outlets we have the kind of shelf space our sales really do not deserve, but he will fight for those outlets to get any special promotions going. Also he is very resistant to losing an account: he hates not to get the benefit, so to speak from his investment.

All of this means that you have to avoid trying to be too directive with Martin. It is best to sow the seed of an idea, let it grow, follow it up later, and in time he will come to accept the idea. When you are directive, his instinctive response is to see the disadvantages: he is quick to see how it will affect his targets and his customers. This is why I have developed this way of floating ideas with him. It is a lot easier to avoid the objections he will raise, especially as most of them will disappear by the next meeting. He likes an argument, so once he has made a point he is liable to defend it.

I know the biscuits are a problem for the salesmen. In many cases they are going into a level of outlet they normally would not cover; to some there is a feeling this is below their status. At this stage there is a lot of work building the product's image and position, which does not get reflected in the volume of sales. Knowing his concerns, I should have taken the opportunity to restate the marketing strategy more positively. I could then have accepted his problems, but still directed the discussion to the outcomes I wanted.

I think the major problem I found with the interview is getting him to talk about what I want him to talk about. I am sure this idea of floating ideas is right, but at times it is not enough. For instance, I have no real idea what he thinks of mail shots, what should be in it and so on. Like most successful salesmen he is skilful about avoiding subjects, if he wants to. So I really should ask more questions. I tend to make statements and wait for a response, which is fine when I want a general reaction, but not directed when I want feedback on a specific point.

This may be the reason why I often feel, when I have meetings with Martin, we spend the greater proportion of the time on his interests. I think it is important that he feels he can raise his interests. I know when I was a salesman it can get very lonely and appear as though nobody in head office or in management is the least bit interested in you or your ideas. However, the balance may not be right. If I could find a way of controlling the meetings better, without stopping him from feeling he can say what he wants, that would be great.

The Salesman's Comments

Our monthly sales meeting was fine. The great thing about David is he has not forgotten what it is like to be a salesman. He is such a nice man and he is genuinely interested in your ideas and opinions. Take for instance our discussion on cakes, we all know the range is old and is not getting any easier to sell. I wish it were different, but it is not. It is hard for us to remain enthusiastic about the product. So it is important we get our moans or concerns about it out of our systems, with each other and not with the customer. David understands that. He is good at distinguishing between genuine grievances or problems and getting things off your chest.

Another example was our discussion on the new biscuit. He listened to my points about displaying the product, and I know he will look into it. Even if it is impractical he will explain the reasons, he does not forget things.

What I also like is the way he involves you in new ideas. I do not like to be presented with *faits accomplis* and he floats his ideas with you. Not only does this give you time to consider the situation and give a reasoned response, but I do feel involved. If I do have a valid point it gets considered, before all the decisions are finalised. I certainly feel I can influence decisions. He keeps you informed. We all guessed that they would go for a savoury individual snack, but it is still nice to have that opinion confirmed.

I know a lot of people might think David is not forceful or direct enough, but I do not agree. Occasionally I have to push him to get a definite answer. His greatest strength is, he was an excellent sales-man and all the salesmen know that. He knows this business, and with his experience you cannot fool him. I know he was not satisfied with my performance on creams or the new accounts, and he did not have to spell it out in great detail for me to get the message. I respect him for that. Everyone has the odd bad month, he does not rub it in, but I know I must not let it continue.

SUMMARY

Throughout this book we have been stressing that successful inter-viewing and managerial communications are dependent upon a number of factors: a clarity of purpose and outcome, establishing an appropriate role and relationship, managing the pressures and influences brought into the interview and the extent to which the interview can be planned. It is vital that a strategy for the interview is developed, which is consistent both with these factors and the skills of the interviewer.

We have commented in this chapter that the model or concept of leadership that a manager has, can also influence his choice of approach. However, if this concept of leadership leads to constantly selecting an inappropriate role, then in the long run highly dysfunc-tional communications with corresponding work problems can develop.

It is the constant reinforcement and modification of behaviours and communication patterns in the regular work review interview rather than the 'special opportunities to communicate', that in the end determine whether a manager's communications are effective.

Familiarity can enhance confidence, but it also breeds habits and complacency. It is, therefore, not a sign of uncertainty to ask the question 'Is the way I want to handle this meeting consistent with what I want to achieve?', but the first step in ensuring that your communications continue to be effective.

This chapter has been written as a summary of the ideas discussed in the book, applying them to regular work reviews. We finish the book in a practical way by providing you with a document which managers have found helpful in preparing themselves for inter-views. We know that if you use it regularly for a short period, the questions will become part of your effective communications.

Manager's Preparation Document

Why do you normally meet or relate to this person?

Is this meeting different? What is the specific purpose of the meeting?

Is there a 'hierarchy' of possible outcomes to the interview? What is the minimum you must achieve? Are you clear what the subsequent outcomes will be, or is that something which the other person will control or influence?

Do you think the person you are seeing will have a similar purpose or outcome? In what ways? Is it similar but conflicting, or different but compatible?

What sort of pressures and influences will you bring into the interview? Which are the pressures which will help you achieve your outcomes? Which will make it difficult for you? Are there any which give you no choice about the outcome?

What pressures are likely to be on the other person? Will they help you or not? Can you use them to achieve your outcomes? If you are not sure what pressures or influences are on them, what questions will you have to ask to find out?

Are there formal or company procedures, which have to be followed? Have you obtained the facts/information that you need? Are there any key facts or opinions that you will have to obtain during the interview?

Does this suggest an appropriate relationship that you must establish in the interview? Do you have any choice? Will it have to change during the interview?

How should you structure and manage the interview?

Do you have to do something at the beginning of the interview to change or establish the other person's expectations?

Should you state the purpose and/or the outcome for this specific interview? Do you need to clarify what the other person hopes to achieve? Are you clear what the structure or sequence of the interview will be? Would it be helpful to outline the sequence to the other person, or should you ask them what items they would like to cover?

Should you start by outlining your own point of view or by asking the other person for theirs?

Do different parts of the interview demand different relationships? Does this suggest that one sequence is better than another? How will you manage the changes in role?

How will you manage the feelings, either your own or the other person's?

What skills are appropriate to managing your and the other person's outcomes and feelings?

Can you identify places during the interview where summaries would be helpful?

Can you finish the interview in a way which will help any subsequent meetings?

Bibliography

American Management Association *Performance Appraisal: A Study of Current Techniques,* 1984.

Argyris, C. *Personality and Organization,* Harper and Row, 1957.

Blanchard, K. and Johnson, S. *The One Minute Manager,* William Morrow, 1982/Collins, 1983.

Bradford, D. and Cohen, A. *Managing for Excellence,* Wiley, 1984.

Bureau of National Affairs *Performance Appraisal Programs,* 1983.

Department of Manpower and Immigration, Saskatchewan *Generic Skills for Occupational Training,* 1983.

DeVries, D. L. et al. *Performance Appraisal on the Line,* Centre for Creative Leadership, 1980.

Handy, Charles *Gods of Management,* Souvenir Press, 1978.

——*Understanding Organisations,* Penguin Books, 3rd edition, 1985.

Hayes and Nutman, *Understanding the Unemployed,* Tavistock, 1981.

Herzberg, Mausner, and Snyderman, *The Motivation to Work,* Wiley, 1958.

Long, Phil *Performance Appraisal Revisited,* Institute of Personnel Management, 1986.

Mintzberg, H. *The Nature of Managerial Work,* Harper and Row, 1973.

Murgatroyd, Stephen *Counselling and Helping,* The British Psychological Society, 1985.

Murray Parkes, Colin *Psycho-social Transitions: A Field for Study,* Social Science and Medicine, vol no. 5, pp. 101–15, 1971.

Peters, Thomas and Waterman, Robert *In Search of Excellence,* Harper and Row, 1982.

Randell, G., Packard, P. and Slater, J. *Staff Appraisal A First Step to Effective Leadership,* Institute of Personnel Management, 1984.

Robinson, Graham. Working Paper, (unpublished course notes), 1988.

Seligman, M. *Helplessness,* W. H. Freeman, 1975.

Stewart, Rosemary *Managers and their Jobs,* Macmillan, 1967, 2nd edition, 1988.

Watson, Goodwin in *The Planning of Change* (chapter 9) page 488, edited by W. Bennis, K. Benne, and R. Chin, Holt, Rinehart, 1974.

Contact Address

Wessex Organization Consultants

Chris Eling and Mike Dutfield are partners in Wessex Organization Consultants. They are experienced in designing and running training courses to improve a person's effectiveness in working with people, for many organisations in the public and private sectors. Most of their training is tailor-made for particular clients, although they also run some public courses.

If you would like to discuss your organisation's training needs, or would like information about particular courses, please contact:

Chris Eling
Wessex Organization Consultants
1, Stoney Lane
Winchester
SO22 6DN
Telephone 0962-883535

Courses and Workshops

Wessex Organization Consultants run courses and workshops on the following subjects:

PERSONAL SKILL DEVELOPMENT

- Interviewing and Counselling Skills
- Appraisal Interviewing
- Selection Interviewing
- Counselling at Work
- Redundancy Counselling
- Assertiveness at Work
- Effective Presentation Skills

WORKING WITH OTHERS

- Communication Improvement
- Working in Successful Teams
- Managing Teams Effectively

TRAINING OF TRAINERS

- Training Skills for the Part-time Trainer
- Mentoring Skills

ORGANISATIONS AND CHANGE

- Organisation Analysis for Improved Effectiveness
- Consultancy Skills Workshops
- Role Review and Change Workshops

QUALITY IMPROVEMENT PROGRAMMES

WORKING WITH CUSTOMERS

- Customer Care Programmes
- Skill Development Workshops for Experienced Sales People

Index

achievement 96
Action Cycle 160–2, 165, 172
American Psychological
    Association 159
appraisal forms 30, 128
Argyris 104
atmosphere 141–3, 163
attitudes 17, 43–9, 50
authority 37, 60

belief systems 131
Bender 123
Blanchard, Kenneth 13
Boston Matrix 133
Bradford, David 174–6
British Civil Service 94
Buber, Martin 41
Bureau of National Affairs 123

career
    issues 126–8
    needs 141
    opportunities 96
Case
    for Advancement 151, 157
    of a Father's Shame 151–2,
        158, 159–60
    of the Missing Orders 150,
        156–7, 160
    of the Missing Report 149–
        50, 155–6
challenges 96

change
    breakthrough change 96–8
    incremental change 96–8
    managing 83–98
    reinforcing 97–8
    resistance to 87–93
    strategies to overcome
        resistance 92–6
Cohen, Alan 174–6
conflicting aims 25
control 12, 30–2, 108, 136, 166,
    167, 205
Counselling and Helping 158
criticism 130–32, 140
culture, organisational 11, 141

Department of Manpower 64
depression, 1930s 101
De Vries 123
difficulties 154–5

educate 93
Eichel 123
emotional appeals 76, 108
empathy 168
ending an interview 22
expectations 43–9

feelings, managing 101, 107–8
force and support 93
formality/informality 76

genuineness 167

Gods of Management 13
grievances 30, 38

habit 87, 93
Handy, Charles 13, 131
heroic style of leadership 175, 176
Herzberg 96, 103, 131
hierarchy of outcomes 136–7, 146, 147, 221
honesty 133, 153

influences 17, 50–63, 111, 127, 140, 221
In Search of Excellence 11, 133
insecurity 88, 93
Institute of Personnel Management 122, 127
interviews
    appraisal 9, 11, 26, 30, 83, 122–48, 165
    career counselling 23–4
    counselling 23–4, 66, 149–73
    disciplinary 23, 24–5, 30, 38–9, 66
    exit 20–2
    management services 24
    personnel 39–40
    policy change 26, 28
    redundancy 24–5, 29, 39, 65–6, 99–121, 164
    selection 67
    termination 24–5, 29
    work review 23, 84, 174–7

Japanese management 124
Johnson, Spencer 13
Jones, Anne 159

Lacho, Stearns and Villere 123
leadership 175–6, 220

management theory 174–6
managers
    demands of the job 141
    pressures and influences on 56–61
Managing for Excellence 174
meaning of work, theories 103–5
'methods' approach 131–2
micro–skills 64
Mintzberg 174
model of interviewing 3, 16–17
motivation 7, 131
Motivation to Work 96
motivators 96
mourning 102
Murgatroyd, Stephen 159

needs 17, 43–9
negotiate 92–3

One Minute Manager 13
openness 127, 145
outcomes 17, 19, 21, 24, 29, 45–6, 48, 62, 72, 85, 93–4, 100–101, 109–11, 135, 136, 142–3, 170, 221

paperless appraisal systems 128
participate 93
perception
    differing 88–9, 93
    selective 25
performance review
    for clerical and blue–collar 128
    purposes of 122–3
    systems 122
Personnel Department 128–9
Peters and Waterman 11, 120, 124, 125

'planability' 29, 32–3
planning
    communication 29–33
    the appraisal interview 135
    the counselling interview 167
    the redundancy interview
        109–11
potential, identification of 123,
    126–7
preparation document 221–2
pressures 50–63, 111, 127, 140,
    221
primacy 87, 93
problems, personal 14, 24–5,
    168–9
procedures 30, 135, 136, 221
profile of your interviews 3, 16
purpose 16, 19–28, 44, 62, 72,
    85, 109, 129–30, 135,
    144, 145, 170, 178, 221

questions, types of
    closed 68
    multiple 69, 194
    open 68
    probing 68
    specific 68

rationality 10, 174
relationship, personal 43, 100
recognition 130–32
redundancy
    and self–image 106
    effect on very ambitious 106
    positive attitude to 105–6
    phases 101–3
respect 133, 134, 167, 171
results 132–3
'results' approach 131–2
rewards 96
Robinson, Graham 94
role
    changing during the

interview 38, 138–9,
    146, 165
appropriate for appraisals
    138–9
overload 36
set 34–5
stress 36
types
    advisory 34, 37, 94, 141,
        164
    consultative 34, 37, 40
    counselling 34, 37, 40, 76,
        164
    executive 34, 36, 39, 60,
        76, 94, 111, 138,
        141, 145–6, 164,
        172–3, 176
    expert 37, 40, 158–60,
        162, 171
    fact–finder 38, 152
    tutorial 34, 37

salary review 123
    linked with performance
        review 123–6, 134
script 29
Seligman 106
self–image, and redundancy
    105–7
self–interest 88, 92–3
skills 17, 64–78, 111–12
    balance of 65, 66, 67
    types
        eliciting information 64,
            68–72, 112
        managing emotion 64, 75–
            7, 112, 168
        feedback 65, 69, 71–2, 73,
            74–5, 112, 127,
            138
        presenting information 64,
            72–5, 111–12, 137,
            205
        summarising 70, 73, 138

status 96
Stewart, Rosemary 1, 8, 14, 174
strategy 25
structure
  combined 147
  for appraisal interviews
          144–8
  for control 31–2
  issue–determined 147, 148
  time–determined 147, 148
style 40, 93–4, 95
subordinates, pressures and
          influences on 51–4
supporting statements 69, 112
SWOT analysis 133

Thinking Cycle 160–62, 165,
          172

time, spent interviewing 1, 8,
          174
trust, lack of 88, 93, 154

uncertainty, managing 142

values 17, 43–9, 50, 73, 76, 99,
          176

'yes but' syndrome 159–60

'Zeus' culture 13